BLOOD IN
YOUR BOOTS

BLOOD IN YOUR BOOTS

Navy SEAL Stories from the Silver Strand (1957–1967)

JOHN RANDALL STEPHENSON, ESQ.

BLOOD IN YOUR BOOTS: Navy SEAL Stories from the Silver Strand (1957–1967)
Copyright © 2023 by John Randall Stephenson, Esq.

All rights reserved. This book or any portion thereof may not be reproduced or used in any manner whatsoever without the express written permission of the publisher, except for the use of brief quotations in a book review.

Printed in the United States of America

Luminare Press
442 Charnelton St.
Eugene, OR 97401
www.luminarepress.com

LCCN: 2023903997
ISBN: 979-8-88679-229-4

DEDICATION

This book is dedicated to all the UDT-SEALs and other persons who provided information, filled in gaps, pieced together stories, read passages, and otherwise graciously helped me write and publish this book. A special thank you is given to John Schmidt, Cathal Flynn, Dan Hendrickson, Franklin Anderson, Ron Bell, Ron and Judy Ethridge, and Jack Couture for their assistance.

This book is also dedicated to all the other officers and enlisted personnel in the early days of the Underwater Demolition Teams and Navy Sea, Air, Land Teams who dedicated their lives, and sometimes gave their lives, to create the modern-day Navy SEAL Teams. I have fond memories of many of them and tremendous respect for all of them.

Finally, a special thank you is given to Anna Shay for her support and assistance in the publication of this book.

CONTENTS

Synopsis xi
Preface xii
*Recollections of Former
Officers and Teammates* xv
"Children of the Wall" xxiii

    CHAPTER I 1
    CHAPTER II 5
    CHAPTER III 12
    CHAPTER IV 16
    CHAPTER V 21
    CHAPTER VI 31
    CHAPTER VII 35
    CHAPTER VIII 45
    CHAPTER IX 49
    CHAPTER X 56
    CHAPTER XI 62
    CHAPTER XII 65
    CHAPTER XIII 68
    CHAPTER XIV 72
    CHAPTER XV 77
    CHAPTER XVI 81
    CHAPTER XVII 86
    CHAPTER XVIII 90
    CHAPTER XIX 95

CHAPTER XX	100
CHAPTER XXI	107
CHAPTER XXII	114
CHAPTER XXIII	119
CHAPTER XXIV	124
CHAPTER XXV	129
CHAPTER XXVI	134
CHAPTER XXVII	141
CHAPTER XXVIII	147
CHAPTER XXIX	150
CHAPTER XXX	154
Conclusion	*157*
Service Record	*159*
The Navy Seal	*163*
Index of Names	*165*
About the Author	*169*

Maxie Stephenson (Vietnam, 1965)
(Source: Personal collection of John Randall Stephenson, Esq. All rights reserved.)

SYNOPSIS

Everyone knows about the Navy SEALs. With their legendary training and history of successful operations, they have become modern-day American heroes. However, little is known publicly about the early days of the Navy SEAL Teams. When were the Teams formed? Who were the original Navy SEALS? How did they become the formidable fighting unit that they are today?

This book tells that story.

It is based upon true events as seen through the eyes and mind of a young officer, Lieutenant Commander John M. "Maxie" Stephenson, Jr., USN. With a broad smile, deep chest, heavy-set jaw and piercing blue eyes, Maxie served as a member of Underwater Demolition Team 12 and Navy SEAL Team One from 1957 to 1967. As the oldest son of a prominent ranching and farming family in Wyoming, who does not even know how to swim when he is drafted into the Navy, the book chronicles Maxie's completion of the famous Navy SEAL training in Coronado, California, and some of the challenges he faced as an officer in the early days of Naval Special Warfare.

The life of each of the early Navy SEALs was a foil of grit and humor. The book depicts the antics of Maxie and his teammates in the early 1960's, their parties, and their exploits with the women who loved them. Also included are many colorful characters, including Lt. John Schmidt, who went on to become a successful physician, Lt. "Whiskey Jack" Sudduth, who helped Maxie train many of the early Navy SEALs, Eric "Fuck" Melnor, who ended up in a Mexican jail with Maxie and helped him escape and swim back to Coronado under Mexican gunfire, and many other characters and stories depicting this little-known period of U.S. Naval history.

PREFACE

As stated in the synopsis, this book consists of a series of stories recorded by my father, Capt. John M. "Maxie" Stephenson, Jr., USNR. He served as an officer in Navy Underwater Demolition Team Twelve (UDT 12) and SEAL Team One from 1957 to 1967, in Coronado, California. The stories are recollections of his early days in the Navy and of becoming a Frogman and SEAL at the U.S. Naval Amphibious Base in Coronado. The stories are often humorous, depicting the colorful lives of the men who completed UDT training with my father in 1959 and who went on to become effective members and operators in UDT 12 and SEAL Team One in the early 1960's.

These are not stories about my father's combat operations in Vietnam and elsewhere. Although he sometimes alludes to his combat operations in the stories, those stories unfortunately died with him after his accidental death in 1982, at the age of 48.

My father recorded these stories in the early 1970's at our house in Reno, Nevada. At the time, he had contacted a published author who was interested in writing a novel using the stories. I recall my father sitting at his desk in our house with a microphone and an old reel-to-reel magnetic tape recorder telling the stories and his recollections and experiences in UDT 12 and SEAL Team One. The recorded stories were later transcribed by his secretary onto long sheets of legal length paper (see following photograph).

> 1
>
> I was remembering H.C. Cunningham's lecture back in training. He said to, in cases like this, get you a great big breath of air and get under the water, if you couldn't do that, try to bump the shark on the nose. Someway or another they must have been sensitive in that part of the body, and then, of course, he said, if that doesn(t work, just hope he only takes one bite and hope he doesn't have a buddy that wanting to come in either. Apparently, however, remembering the same lecture, the shark doesn't necessarily like to eat the human body. After he makes one pass, and of course, if they're not traveling in a wolfpack, cases of a lone shark, as this appeared to be the case, they would only make one pass most probably, and go on about his business. Also, the type of shark, the breed of shark and the area of the world or waters, temperature of waters, and the living conditions that the shark lives in also, I remember, would have an affect on his verocity. So, I didn't have time to get that big breath of air, didn't seem like I wanted to go underwater without my mouthpiece in my mouth, or the valve, which had been screwed down on my air tank, shut, In fact, all I had time to do was reach out and bump the shark as hard as I could with the balls of my open hand on the nose. Los and behold, it worked. The old boy turned and I can remember he hit Ed and knocked him into me, and left. However, it was still over an hour before the submarine would return and we had a long, long wait. A And I can remember being at least 6 feet away from Ed and could see his eyeballs were as big as two silver dollars, and I'm sure mine were as big as two coffee cu saucers. Finally, the sub returned. In this case we had a sounding devise which indicated he was making a sound for us to return an underwater sonar sound so that he could receive in his sonar equipment our sound and attempt to pick us up, and as I have stated earlier, being picked up in a submarine is a rather hard task, and particularly at night. This happened to be one
> usually it's 5 to 6 feet away

After my father's accidental death in 1982, the stories went missing for many years. Then, approximately 34 years after the stories were recorded, Stan Rand, my father's former accountant and fellow Navy reserve officer in Reno, mailed me a letter indicating that he had found several boxes of my father's tax documents. In the boxes, Stan said he had found the transcripts of the stories and thought that I would like to have them. I gratefully accepted the offer.

John Randall Stephenson, Esq.

The main hurdle I had in finishing the stories was that, although I had grown up around many of my father's officers and teammates, I was never a member of any SEAL team, nor had I ever tried to become one. My father had never pressed military service on me, including any type of service in Naval Special Warfare. He raised me and my sister, Janell, in Nevada where we learned to ski, backpack, ride horses and work cattle on ranches. Despite this hurdle, however, these stories have miraculously become published as my father wished so many years ago. It could not have been done without the help of so many of his former officers and teammates, many of whom I remember as a child in Coronado and whose recollections of my father I have included in this book.

I would like to make a few comments about race relations and my father's use of racial terms that may be perceived as insensitive or incorrect under our current social norms. In writing this book, I did not change any questionable statements made by my father. I did this to remain historically accurate and to ensure that the reader has a sense of what was considered to be acceptable during my father's era. Both of my parents were very progressive for their day and, as a family, we were told that black persons were the same as us and should always be treated that way. We were also told that if any of my father's friends or any other Frogman or SEAL who was black came to our house, we should give them great respect because they may save our father's life in combat someday. I am grateful that I was raised this way.

Finally, I would like to note that I did not publish this book for money. I published it for the members of my family, and for the historical value these stories confer upon the early development of the Navy SEAL Teams and Naval Special Warfare. I hope all persons enjoy reading this book, and I especially hope the readers catch a glimpse into a fascinating chapter of U. S. Naval history.

RECOLLECTIONS OF FORMER OFFICERS AND TEAMMATES

The following stories and recollections of Maxie Stephenson have been included to confer upon the reader a better understanding of who Maxie Stephenson was and how he was perceived in UDT 12 and SEAL Team One. Overall, he was considered a highly effective officer and operator in UDT 12 and SEAL Team One. He was also extremely competitive and known for his humor and antics.

Admiral Cathal L. Flynn, USN

Cathal Flynn was the first Navy SEAL to become an Admiral. Admiral Flynn later was the first Admiral from the Teams to "run a desk" in the Pentagon. According to Admiral Flynn, Maxie Stephenson was recommended for promotion to the rank of Commodore in June of 1982 (see attached recommendation for promotion to Commodore). The rank of Commodore was considered to be a flag officer back then.

Admiral Flynn was called "Irish" in the Teams because he was a native of Dublin, Ireland. Irish went through training in Virginia, which is where SEAL Team Two was located. In those days, the trainees from Virginia were sent to Coronado to complete the SCUBA portion of the training. Maxie was an instructor in the training unit together with the main instructor, Kevin Murphy. Irish completed his diving training under Maxie.

According to Irish, Maxie was immensely strong, with a big chest and intimidating smile. One could never tell what Maxie was thinking when he smiled at you. He was, however, known as an exceptional officer in UDT 12 and SEAL Team One.

Maxie had a connection with the enlisted men which was unusual for an officer. They looked up to him as one of them and was an officer whom they would follow. This was a great asset in the Teams.

Irish stated that Maxie had a propensity to eat electric light bulbs as a party trick. However, although Maxie was always the life of UDT and SEAL Team parties in Coronado, he, like other members of the teams, had a wife and children to whom he was dedicated at the time.

As to going through UDT training, Irish stated that a usual practice at the time among the officers who were going through Hell Week together was to have an informal agreement to work together to help each other and their boat crews. This practice was known as "cooperate to graduate." But Maxie was too competitive for that and was in competition with several other officers during training. Even after successfully completing UDT training, he would have brutal, legendary foot races with the other officers.

A man named Jim Barnes was the Commanding Officer (CO) of SEAL Team One at the time. He and Maxie, as the Executive Officer (XO) of SEAL Team One, operated together in the Rung Sat Special Zone in Vietnam. This was an area of Vietnam where the Teams engaged in various non-advisory, combat operations. Jim Barnes apparently relied upon Maxie to train men for combat operations in the Rung Sat Special Zone. Maxie also carried out combat operations there. He was then promoted to the rank of Lieutenant Commander and later Commander in SEAL Team One.

Irish felt that Maxie was one of the few officers at the time who understood that the overall function and effectiveness of the SEAL Teams was not limited to operations in Vietnam. He believed the purpose of the SEAL Teams was much broader than that and future operations would take the Teams into areas all over the world. It turned out that Maxie was correct in this regard.

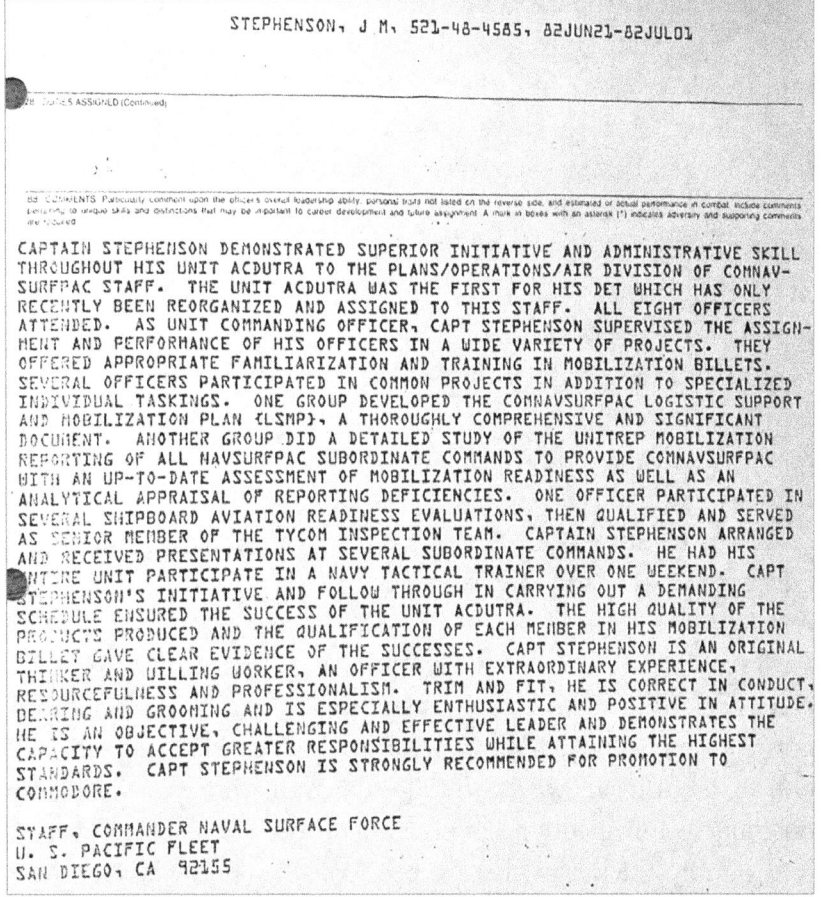

Recommendation for Promotion to Commodore—Maxie Stephenson

Commander Franklin Anderson, USN

Franklin Anderson was the former Commanding Officer (CO) of SEAL Team One in the early 1960's. Maxie was Franklin's Executive Officer (XO). According to Franklin, he and Maxie worked well together and accomplished several goals to improve the functioning and combat operations of SEAL Team One in Vietnam and other areas of southeast Asia. The following statements are directly from Franklin.

John Randall Stephenson, Esq.

"I remember Maxie Stephenson well. I was in the Class of 1956 at Colorado State University (then Colorado A & M) together with him. He later came into the Teams as an officer in Underwater Demolition Team 12. He then went into SEAL Team One. He was the XO when I came back from Vietnam."

"He and I worked on the SPECWAR Staff (then Naval Operational Support Group, Pacific), and together we worked very closely in rewriting the NAVAL WARFARE PUBLICATIONS (NWP's) for the SEAL Teams. Also, one of our most successful accomplishments together was a rewrite of the Manpower Authorization for SEAL Team One. We jumped it up to 500 people. Everyone said we were crazy, but in the long run it proved out that we were correct in increasing the manpower of the SEAL Teams."

"I left the SPECWAR Staff and took over as the Commanding Officer of SEALS, and Maxie was my Executive Officer. We worked very well together and made significant changes to the SEAL Teams."

"I remember one incident vividly. A man named Jerry Bush had come back from Vietnam and was getting into trouble. He had also gotten into trouble in Vietnam but Jim Barnes, his Commanding Officer, let him get away with it. I learned that Jerry was planning on going to Coronado to a bar during on-duty hours. I told Maxie to drop into the bar to check it out. We wrote Jerry up and eventually shit-canned him because of his constant behavior problems."

"Maxie was a rough, tough hombre. One time Lieutenant Ron Smith was screwing around, and Maxie tried to pick a fight with him. Suddenly, Ron just disappeared. No guts."

"I also recall that when Maxie first got out of the Navy in 1962, he went back to the family ranch in Wyoming and was feeding cattle for the market when the market dropped. So, he then began butchering the cattle and brought them to California to sell. (His major in college at Colorado A & M was Animal Nutritionist.) Later he got into the explosives business and bought into the company. He was doing great until Dupont saw he was in competition with them and stopped his source of supplies."

"I could go on about the things Maxie would do. He would eat glass or do just about anything else on a dare or bet."

"I still cannot believe he ran out of air and died while diving, but the fellows he was with were all good people. Accidents do happen to the best of us. I knew Maxie probably better than anyone in the Navy."

"Attached are a couple of photos. One photo is with Craig Dorman on a submarine planning an operation with Maxie. The other inset photo was taken at a party given by Maynard Weyers. Lance Mann is on the extreme left, then Maynard Weyers with the hat and Maxie with the patch. I am located under his raised arm."

Planning an Operation (Maxie Stephenson in center. Vietnam, 1965). Inset: Lance Mann, Maynard Weyers, Franklin Anderson, and Maxie Stephenson, Coronado, California (1966)
(Source: Personal Collection of John Randall Stephenson, Esq. All Rights Reserved.)

Commander Ron Bell, USN

Ron Bell was an officer in SEAL Team One under Maxie. After completion of his duties at the Naval Amphibious Base in Coronado, Ron learned one of the various Indonesian languages and was assigned as an attaché in Washington, D.C.

Ron completed Navy SEAL training in Coronado, California, when Maxie was in the instructor unit there. Ron stated that Maxie was known in the Teams as being highly competitive amongst his teammates. He would never quit no matter what the assignment was. Ron said he would never have wanted to be in a fight with Maxie because he would just not quit until one of them was unconscious or dead.

Maxie is still a legend in the Teams according to Ron. He is remembered for his leadership and willingness to see the job through regardless of the challenges he faced.

Maxie was also famous for eating glass. He would win money by making bets that he could eat glass. He also occasionally ate horse manure on a bet. One night while driving back from Mexico, he and several other guys bet that he would not eat horse manure. They stopped somewhere in Imperial Beach which had horses. Maxie apparently found horse manure that was sufficiently fresh and won the bet.

Although known for his wild antics, Ron stated that Maxie was a highly competent and effective officer in SEAL Team One, and Ron trusted him completely in combat. There were few men he trusted more.

Ron Ethridge, Enlisted, USN

Ron Ethridge served as an enlisted member of UDT 11 at roughly the same time Maxie served in UDT 12 (1959—1967).

Ron recalled playing football in the UDT's with Maxie. As mentioned in this book, the UDT football games often resulted in "accidents" such as broken noses, broken limbs, and missing teeth. Ron recalled Maxie participating joyously in those games.

Although Maxie rarely told combat stories, Ron relayed one story wherein Maxie was serving on a combat mission in Vietnam, probably around 1965-66. At the time, Maxie and other members of UDT 12 and SEAL Team One were developing the early guerrilla warfare tactics that were later incorporated into their standard operating procedures.

According to Ron, on various night operations in Vietnam, Maxie and the other members of his team would strike the Vietnamese soldiers swiftly and hard, thereby maximizing the element of surprise. After conducting several such operations, a particular CIA officer insisted that Maxie prepare a report setting forth the number of soldiers killed or injured during the operations. Because the tactics used during the operations involved fast strikes and quick exits after the strikes, body counts were not conducted and were a significant impediment to the success and safety of the operation. However, the CIA officer insisted on body count reports. Maxie, being somewhat resistant to such orders, apparently complied by taking the bodies of the Vietnamese soldiers killed after a strike and piling the bodies up on a river raft. The raft was then floated to an appropriate location for the CIA officer to count the bodies himself. The not-so-subtle message sent on the raft was that the top body on the pile had a United States flag shoved up his ass. No further demands for body counts were made by that CIA officer.

Ron and his wife Judy later settled in Reno at the same time we were living there in 1968. Maxie and Ron remained good friends and I recall many dinners and visits with my parents and Ron and Judy Ethridge. I learned to bartend and mix cocktails at these gatherings. Those are skills that I enjoy having to this day.

Lord Mountbatten (Left) Observing Ron Ethridge (Third from Left). U.S. Naval Amphibious Base, Coronado, California (1961)

(Source: Personal collection of John Randall Stephenson, Esq. All rights reserved.)

"CHILDREN OF THE WALL"

I have included the following poem written by Karen Horn, whose father was killed in action in Vietnam in 1968. He served as the XO (Executive Officer) of UDT 12 after Maxie Stephenson.

The poem speaks for itself. I have included it simply as a reminder that a Frogman or Navy SEAL, or any other sailor or soldier for that matter, does not consist solely of himself or herself. Wives, husbands, children, and other family members are also part of him or her, and, when lost, he or she is never replaced.

> We are the children of the Wall
> That is what we are,
> One and all;
> Children of men now gone,
> But whose memories linger on.
>
> That is all we have to cling to,
> That is why we make do;
> We live life day by day,
> Wondering what our fathers would say.
>
> If the paths we have chosen are right,
> Do they justify our fathers' deadly fight;
> Did they give their lives in vain,
> Were ours untouched by their pain?

John Randall Stephenson, Esq.

I think not—they would be proud,
No matter how many a gray cloud;
Whatever we may choose to do,
Their love will always ring true.

Sons and daughters of men who took the fall,
We are the children of the Wall.

(Copyright 1993. All rights reserved)

CHAPTER I

In Maxie's own words…

If this ever makes a book, I desire it to be a satire on the man who makes a Frogman and SEAL—his love, his life, his desires, his background, and who he is. He's been a tremendous character, a tremendous individual to be around. Throughout my life of getting to know this individual, become a part of him, a part of it, I, at no time, desire to prostitute the future of this organization; the future of the individual, nor the idea that he represents. It is necessary however, to try to portray this in the best interest of him, his life, his country, his god, his woman, his Navy.

Throughout my college career at Colorado A&M (now Colorado State at Fort Collins), I had absolutely no desire to ever become a part of the military. I had no ideas or intentions toward this. I grew up in a small town in Wyoming, called Lingle, taking part in every portion of it—4-H, livestock, athletics, livestock judging team, met the girl who is now my wife, and went to college with the sincere desire to learn all about the animal proper that I ever knew. I always intended to return to Wyoming, the ranch, and proceeded with an intense desire to do such while in college.

I can remember my father when I first started to school saying, "Son, those college professors are good. There's a lot to be learned, but it's not all in those books. You've got to get around, see a little bit, participate a little bit, and work in that manner." As it turned out, I, being somewhat inclined athletically, desired to play football. This became a rather difficult situation, coming from a small school, never playing the game, seeing only two college games in my life, trying to make a college team. We procured a suit, I went out, and was one of eleven out of sixty-some fellas or more to go up to the varsity squad. From there I went and had not a dynamic, but adequate football career. I also participated in track, livestock judging teams, and rodeo.

Maxie Stephenson on the Family Ranch in Wyoming (1963)
(Source: Personal collection of John Randall Stephenson, Esq. All rights reserved.)

Navy Enlistment

When I was a sophomore in high school, I met the woman I am still married to, Rosemary Weitzel.

Upon completion of college, graduating with a degree in animal nutrition, I proceeded back to our family ranch in Wyoming where I intended to spend the rest of my life. I went on to go about the business of ranching.

Suddenly, throughout this part of the situation, I was informed that I was eligible for the draft at the last end of the Korean War, and it was necessary to get a military obligation out of the way. My father, Mel Stephenson, talked this over with me, and we went on to discuss what we could do about it. I guess for no other reason that I know of, we just went at the thing in what we called a logical manner, dragging my feet all the way, I thought the Navy would be the best because they always gave you a good plate of beans and had a clean bed at night, which I was later to find out that this was not always the case.

So, one day I loaded up a load of sheep to take to the livestock market in Denver and, as it turned out, sold the sheep. Manure all over my boots—if you've ever smelled the sheep smell, you can tell that I wouldn't have been what you call an ideal candidate for Naval Officer's Candidate School (OCS).

I went on into the recruiting office in Denver, Colorado, somewhere around March 1957, and explained that I wanted to join the Navy. They gave me the normal set of application forms, and I started filling them out. When I got down to the point of education, I noticed that there were only places for twelve years of schooling, and, because I had completed 4 years of college at Colorado A&M in 1956, I went ahead and put in sixteen. I returned the application to the individuals. I did notice a rather attractive secretary there, so I felt a little bit embarrassed about my clothing and attire. However, she noticed that I had a college degree, and proceeded to explain to me that I should be a naval officer candidate. Well, I agreed with her. It was tremendous that she helped me in that manner.

They brought out an officer and talked to me awhile and gave me the normal pep talk. I then went ahead and filled the forms to do some kind of IQ test. I hate tests, always have. Normally, I did very lousy on them. When the officer saw the grade and said I had a very minute chance to make the Navy, I, of course, being naïve and not too knowledgeable of the situation, just knew that I was going to the Navy. I had no idea what the situation was, what I was going to do or how. I talked extensively to the man to try to get him to listen, to tell him that I did have some background. I thought I could do it; I'd never been defeated that I know of, totally. Maybe the first time, but hardly the second time, in my life. I like to be a fairish competitor; I like to do a good job.

He gave me some forms to fill out, saying it would depend primarily on the character recommendations of the individuals to whom I sent the forms. I sent a form to the United States Senator from Wyoming who was personal friend of my father's. The Governor of Wyoming was also a personal friend of my father's, so he received a form too. Finally, I sent forms to one of my coaches and to an old sheepherder I knew many, many years ago. I got them on the ball, and they followed up with good recommendations which I got back. As a result, I was called on May 1, 1957, to come down to Denver. I had been accepted to be sworn in. Little did we realize that this was the only the initial process. We thought that by being sworn in that it was good-bye forever, so in a period of about four hours one morning we closed all my business on the ranch, headed to Denver with my father, my wife, Rosemary, and our new-born daughter, Janell. They swore us in, and finally he said, "Well, you report here Monday, and we'll fly you to Newport, Rhode Island." I said, "I'm ready to go now." And it happened to be on a Friday, so he said, "Would you like to go to Washington, D.C.?" I couldn't believe it, it was like all my life you read books and study about things, and there we were. He got a ticket to Washington, D.C. A few hours later, on the plane, I was like a gawky little kid seeing all these great things. Even though I was somewhat of a grown man, you could have given me a sucker and I would have been very happy. I was seeing all the historical things where our country came from. I had a good time in the city and was presented my first temptation to find other women. However, I passed that up, and the same weekend headed up to Newport, Rhode Island. Actually, we went to Providence, Rhode Island, and took a train down to Newport and checked in. On the way down I met several people, and one of them I remember was Ken Sansburn. He still is a friend of mine.

CHAPTER II

Officer's Candidate School

So, on May 3, 1957, I started going through Officer's Candidate School. I was very intrigued. I can remember the first time I saw an aircraft carrier go up the bay, through the little harbor there. I couldn't believe that such a huge thing could float on such a small body of water. I found OCS to be challenging, very interesting, and perfect for the non-military, the ornery kid, non-conformist, as we would term it today. I had other terms for myself then. I proceeded to go about the business of becoming a naval officer. However, my first observation of my contemporaries was somewhere along the line I was behind the tree. They used big words and threw their degrees around. I thought that I knew absolutely nothing, and, of course, I was running with a few missing spark plugs in my mind, because I felt that since mentally, I hadn't provided myself with a very good a start through my testing, that these guys were outstandingly sharp. But, as I studied them longer and longer, I found out that they were a bunch of pseudo-bastards in my mind, and that they didn't have the background, the responsibilities, or the make-up that I had come to determine that I had. However, it so seemed that always hung around me. It seemed that I offered strength, whatever it was, and in later years that analysis of that individual, how to be around him and how to work with him, paid off, but when I went on to work with some of the, what we would call, regular-type naval officers, which I found that I liked and got along with very well. This was the start of a long career.

One day while at OCS, and because of the individuals that I thought I would be associating with the next three years and three years only—three years, four months, including OCS—one day they were offering various programs and it appeared you could go and do whatever you so desired. Of course, the big push was to—the Navy sails ships, and ships go to sea—select a ship and get the background so that you would be in position to someday, and as I always do anytime I go to work for anything, be an Admiral. So, I was looking at various programs, they had various subjects that you could attend, and one day they had a mass assembly of all officer candidates. At that time, we were given a presentation by an Underwater Demolition Team (UDT) officer from Little Creek, Virginia.

I immediately identified with this guy. He had everything I thought a man wanted or needed. I had heard and maybe seen—I don't think I ever saw a movie on the guys—that they were pretty tough, and if you could be part of them or with them, you could probably call yourself a man. So, we went ahead and studied the program awhile and talked it over with my wife through correspondence. After that I decided I would try it. I couldn't swim, had no idea how to (this will come out later in other stories), but we, at that time. could not go directly to the underwater demolition training from OCS. However, I did select in my request the west coast, and the training would be conducted in Coronado, California.

Graduation from OCS (1957)
(Source: Personal collection of John Randall Stephenson, Esq. All rights reserved.)

Ordered to Sea After Officer's Candidate School

In 1957, when I got my orders, we were required to spend some time at sea regardless of what school or whatever we did. At the time it didn't look like a very good deal, but in retrospect it was. I did gain a good part of knowledge that I think helped me later in my

UDT-SEAL career. However, at that time, the thought of going to a ship did not enthuse me that much because I had started to get the mental attitude to try to become one of these individuals, still knowing absolutely nothing about the man. As it turned out going to the ship was good experience, and perhaps not having had those few months on the ship—fifteen to be exact—I would never have come in contact with the individual, study the situation, learn it, prepare myself to go to this training, and perhaps wouldn't have given myself the chance to get through it that I did through my shipboard experience.

USS Cavallaro

So, I was ordered to an APD (All-Purpose Destroyer), a small destroyer, which had been converted to carry approximately 100 troops. Throughout my career the sole purpose of this ship, although having many, many tussles with several commanding officers of these vessels, was to support a UDT group (although at this date there were not too many APD's in commission, if any). So we went to Long Beach, California, aboard the USS Cavallaro APD L28 to assume the duties of a new ensign on a ship.

Seasick

While aboard the USS Cavallaro, I had several experiences which should be mentioned as background. It started out, more or less, that I came aboard just before we deployed to sea and was given an interim set of orders to the ship with further duty to UDT training at the convenient starting date which, at that time, appeared to be somewhere throughout the period of time we would be overseas. As it turned out, while we were overseas, it was probably inefficient for the Navy to send me back and get me on, so I stayed aboard longer than I desired. So, then we left Long Beach to head out to sea to deploy to the far west Pacific Ocean. We were not over a day or two out of the port, and I can remember the apprehension that I had of the leaving of a life that I had—it appeared to me that I was going in a backward direction in life. From the ranch to somewhere at a point beyond nowhere. However, this is where we were and what we were to do.

It wasn't long before all these thoughts disappeared quite rapidly after we got into some rough seas. The ship was rolling and pitching and tossing. I seemed to be doing quite well until we were up on the bridge and the Officer of the Deck, I happened to be the Junior Officer of the Deck, became sick and started to get nauseated. I, of course, became the same way. I proceeded to my quarters, called the troop officers' quarters, and was lying there with the dry heaves, when all of a sudden, I could smell this intense smell. This smell later became a part of my life. It seems like the first day at sea the Navy always has some kind of greasy pork chops. I smelled this greasy pork chop smell and looked up and there was a Gunner's Mate Chief named Gruger. I had noticed that he was laughing intensely and had attached a pork chop to the bunk. It was swinging in a very convenient location so that I would observe this horrible thing every time I opened my eyes. Naturally, getting a very, very intense attack of nausea, all of a sudden, I had the thought that I couldn't get any worse, and mentally the whole program turned around for me. I began laughing, seemed like I got well immediately, and never was sick since.

We later pulled into Hawaii. It was a great thrill to get there. I knew I was going to get to see a couple of friends that I had while playing football in college. However, it didn't turn out that way. I spent the rest of my time over there on the ship. However, while on our first day of liberty we were to pay a visit to a Canadian destroyer. Of course, American naval vessels have never been allowed to have alcoholic beverages aboard the ships, however, we were being escorted and doing maneuvers with a squadron of Canadian destroyers and we would all make a token visit aboard one of these destroyers. While aboard, we were allowed to have a few drinks in one of the ward rooms. As it turned out, after having a few drinks, I got into an arm-wrestling match and a few other rather physical activities with the XO (Executive Officer) of one of the ships. After this, I was rather ostracized by my Commanding Officer and Executive Officer and told to return to my ship where I remained.

There were several incidences that did occur after we got overseas; we picked up the first group of UDT men. This was when I got to observe them and observe their situation. We had several liberties with them, and they started to give me the big play on getting through basic training. It appeared that the thing that was most important was the desire -- you had to want to do it, and the word quit became a very, very elemental problem in my mind. Two or three incidences I can remember while carrying these Frogmen aboard the ship: One: I can remember we did an operation called "Strongback" in the Philippines in Dinagyang Bay, and they went in to reconnoiter the beach (I'll go into the missions and what they did later). They did a swim on the beach and so on and so forth, and I was fortunate enough to talk the XO into letting me go. They had a beach charting party, and I noticed that it was a rather large party, seemed to be rather strange that a group that swam in the water, swam under combat and fire on enemy beaches, would send this many people in on the beach. But, as it turned out, they were going in to line up the concession stand, so to speak. There would probably be somewhat of a return to them. Either money or trading goods or barter that could come about, plus arranging a party which later became something that was traditional. This was a consistent conflict with the ship's crew that we were working with and ourselves.

However, the point was that when the Marines or whomever first touched shore there would be Filipino girls there, and men selling Cokes and watermelon and what-have-you. Of course, there would be a little exchange situation with some Frog who was designated at that time as "lifesaver". We'd be over raking in whatever the previous negotiations may have been. Later, I remember about that time going back to Okinawa from the Philippines, I happened to, we had what I called was a rather paranoid CO (Commanding

Officer), I hadn't really gotten to understand the man—never did, in fact—or at that time who a Captain really is and the cold position that an individual in this responsible position really is in. However, getting back to going back to Okinawa, I was given a test called A Day's Work in Navigation. Somehow or another I became the clown at that time among our group in the wardroom. I had been doing various charting programs which I think we had ourselves plotted in the middle of the Sahara Desert and all the officers were coming by and watching my work and it became somewhat of a conversation piece. So, one day, about halfway between the Philippines and Okinawa, the skipper asked after dinner to see my chart. Most of the officers had the presence of mind to get up and leave the wardroom, but I broke into an outrageous laugh. Naturally, he didn't understand what the problem was. I was confined to my quarters.

By this time, I had been elevated to the position of a stateroom in the aft part of the ship just over the screws, which I loved very dearly. It was a very nostalgic place, out-of-the-way place, and it was good quarters. However, being down there the time that I was trying to figure out what to do, reading books, I decided to get the Corpsman to give me a visit to see if I could talk him into sending me a five-gallon can of ethanol, grain alcohol, which had been made by the alcohol-narcotics inventory officer. I had noticed that there was an extra can of this material and had it sent to the stateroom. I called up and had a machinist mate get another can with a spout on it which I transferred the contents of one can into the other. It became the life of luxury to be what we called "put in hack". Again, I guess being part of my opportunistic tendencies, we ended up having the steward's mate serving me Coke by the gallon down there, and all the officers coming down, and there were parties in this back room going on by the hour even including the XO. This also made the CO rather irritated, to the point where I think he finally forgot me. That's the only thing that—as the cliché goes—if he didn't look at it, it would go away.

CHAPTER III

Nickname "Maxie"

However, getting back to Japan and being somewhat ostracized in the ranks of the naval officers, I decided to make friends with some of the enlisted men, which I knew wasn't right, and later I can say that it's a mistake. But this is where I got my nickname "Maxie". I had a lot of energy to burn up when we got to shore and it seemed like it was a great challenge, and then, of course, I wanted to try to indicate to those Frogmen on board that I could be one of them. However, I really could not be without going through the training and going through the fraternal organization as it truly is, because I feel that there's no greater or deeper fraternal order in the world today than this organization. Despite this, however, we would often get over in the clubs and bars such as Yakuska, Sasabo, Chenenkuria, in Korea, White Beach in Okinawa, and other bars and clubs in Hong Kong.

On these excursions it became a game to try to start a bar fight and then see how long you could last, and how you could master this type of fighting, this game. Naturally, during my first few experiences with it I got my clock cleaned. I thought I was pretty tough and could handle anyone that I had run onto thus far, but when it comes to breaking chairs, throwing beer bottles around, using whatever weapon that may be necessary, it's a new game, and normally the enlisted men would bring me back rather unconscious, taking several days to heal up, and nurse my wounds. Through this

I think—I don't know whether the enlisted men put it on me, I don't feel I was ever ostracized by them, but then again—who knows. But through this in the wardroom, a friend named John Thurber gave me the name "Slapsy Maxie". Then, of course, they started calling me "Max" because there were five other men named John in our wardroom. After that, I went on to pick up the name "Maxie". Since some of the members of the UDTs were aboard our ship, they never knew me by anything else other than Maxie.

Underwater Demolition Team Training

Finally, I returned to the States and very soon after arriving, along about the last part of 1958 and turn of 1959, I received that long-awaited set of orders, after some technique that perhaps wasn't right, probably got somewhat a wrong start in the Navy of doing things and asking questions later. However, I found that the phone call had immediate effects, and I received orders for underwater demolition training to start in March, April, or May of 1959. I remember I had 60 days of training and time to train.

Somewhere along the line I never learned to really swim. I'm sure I could get on a pair skis or dogpaddle around long enough to be classified under any normal conditions as a non-swimmer. So, I conducted an intensive campaign, thinking I had the ability to learn and later came to know that this is something that takes many, many years to master. And really was classified, in fact, the day I reported aboard for training, I got the usual PT (physical training) test, which I could do quite well in, and the soaring test. I remember H. O. Cunningham, who was from Kansas, and had a typical Kansas approach, friendly as of all the Kansans I've ever known, coming up and saying, "Son, you're a pretty good-looking specimen, but I'm sure you've got orders somewhere else. You can't swim, and that is what this organization does." So, after getting dressed, and somehow or another procuring a set of orders and showing it to him, he said,

"Good luck." However, from that day on he took an interest in me, and an interest in my career in the UDT's.

Leaving H. O. Cunningham for a minute, I'd like to kind of go back. I left a period out of the story after retuning on the ship stateside that I thought might be something that would be a little different. Continuing my process of trying to identify myself, basically it was a period of testing, testing myself against these UDT guys.

We had several stateside operations at Rocky Shoals up around Monterey, California. I remember it being a very beautiful area, still on a ship yet, and by this time we'd had a new CO, and somehow or another I'd become the golden-haired boy, could handle the ship, given all the responsibilities of shipboard duty, and could take the ship as qualified Officer of the Deck underway. I remember this same Chief Gruger one day wanting to fish, and we were at sea doing some sea trials with the ship characteristics of its turning etc., so on and so forth, and Chief Gruger came up on deck and asked if I could slow the ship down so he could fish. So, I positioned the lookouts to look for schools of fish, and when we found one, we'd take the ship over, and I'd hold the fantail out so that the good Chief could fill his creel full of fish. This same CO, Layton Spidone, who just quite frankly is a man's man, been a WWII skipper, this was his fifth shipboard command, and just an outstanding individual in all respects, had kind of more or less taken me under his wing, and my energies were directed totally in a constructive manner at this time. He had noticed or had discussed or thought that I wanted to go on to be something to be pretty tough and he said one of the few individuals—very, very few individuals—who could lift a 55-pound dummy projectile forward gun mount 5-inch gun on the ship and put it behind his head and do a sit up. Well, at first, I couldn't do too many, but I could do it, so I kept kind of piddling around with this projectile and doing more and more and more. The skipper, Captain Spidone, would kind of bait, so to speak, the CO or Officer In Charge (OIC) of a UDT detachment for their mess bell, and perhaps there would be a little bit of money after we got done doing the pool shark business on them, but I got up to where I could do probably 15 to 20 of them. I think the most I ever remember doing in these types of competitions was 20. You can't believe the money we kind of took care of, and it was kind of nice. I was made the wardroom mess officer handling all the monies, and this did come in handy, when we had various functions to take care of—we had a few extra dollars in our mess treasury, we could put on a pretty good shindig if necessary.

Also, I can remember one time later going into Jim Barnes who now is in Washington, D.C., the Senior Officer in UDT. He was the Officer In Charge at that time, but I can remember pulling into Monterey to do a recon just off the beach by Fort Ord, and there were shark fins. I could not believe it—they were just all over. In fact, later in the day the CO was fishing, and his captain very near the place where the UDT's were going their reconnaissance in the beach area. He was pulling up fish and the sharks were eating them before he could get them aboard. I thought this really took some—again, I had to take some serious thought as to going into this program. I can remember several years later discussing this with Jim, and all I can remember him saying, he's a very cool individual, he said, "What sharks?" and that was about it.

CHAPTER IV

Pre-Training Apprehension and UDT Instructors

Back to H. O. Cunningham and the instructors. Naturally, as you report aboard a new situation, people are there getting ready, and there's the normal talk and the stories going around and the individuals and the apprehensions and the tensions that come with attempting to do something that's unknown, because nobody knows whether they're going to make it. Usually, one out of four to five individuals makes it through this training. I can remember the instructors—there was Mike Parker, who we later called Black Mike. He was a sincere individual, but weird in his ways, and we didn't consider him a strong leader, but in his own right a very talented man. Under him was Al Price, later to be called the Tree Trunk. He had gone to school at Tufts College in Boston and had run the Boston Marathon several times. Of course, the stories build up. Then there was Chief Antrim, Stan Antrim, who was a very domineering, regular-Navy type individual. He was very good looking, and physically extremely strong, with tremendous bearing. And we had Kevin Murphy, an outstanding individual, way above average in intelligence, who had an extremely good command of the English language. Rusty Campbell was a Gunner's Mate, just a tremendous type of man to draw a little inspiration to. There was Clancy, Chief Clancy, another Gunner's Mate, and an Officer named Harvey Hiver, we called him Klondike Ike. He had the most sadistic laugh anybody would ever want to hear. This was the crew into whose hands I was ready to throw my life.

Basic Training Begins

Commencing basic training, the first three weeks of it is primarily running, swimming, calisthenics, and rubber boat work—a half day each in each case. In the morning we had the PT program, extremely strenuous, enough to get the normal man or anybody that wouldn't be properly prepared for this totally exhausted for an entire day. Then we would start out on runs. Runs were in the sand dune area, starting out at perhaps one mile, running, stopping, running, stopping, continually circling back to pick up the stragglers. One of the things the instructors would always totally impress on us, we would line up in columns of two, instructors in front, normally Al Price the marathon runner, and extremely brilliant man along with it, would always say that he didn't ever want to see anybody pass him or touch him or inhibit the instructor in any way. However, he wanted us all right behind him when he got there, wherever it was we were going to stop. Naturally the instructor has the mental advantage of knowing when he's going to stop, and we never did. It was always to anyone's advantage to run up in the front and try to follow the footprint of the instructor as best as possible. This became the envious position and one that would tend to take a rational individual and become irrational in trying to seek this position. Then they would run us into the water and the beach and get us full of sand and mud, and if you were maybe—spirit, spirit, this was something I could always say about training is that I can remember back in my fraternity days in college there was some hazing as we called it or harassment, but basically the instructors always treated us as men. The jobs were tough, they were obtainable, but they were always beyond your comprehension and mentality. This was the way to get through this training. You had to take one day at a time, because if you tried to put the whole thing into focus, to conceive of your doing it, it was impossible. (Much the way I think about this book, by the way.) However, we would go on the runs in the morning, or perhaps in the afternoon.

Then we would go to the pool with our strawberries, groin rots, belt from the sand and various blisters, etc., on your feet from running. We always ran in what we called boon dockers or field shoes. The instructor had the privilege of wearing swim trunks, and, of course, he could, and most of them did, wear boots. (I later found when I became instructor that this gave us more support.) We would then go to the pool and go through the very, very elemental basics of swimming. This is where I started to have my difficulties in swimming. I had a goal to obtain that's not too hard to obtain normally among a community of swimmers. A mile to swim in the pool in 60 minutes is a very easy goal to obtain. I came to think but wasn't really aware of the fact that I can't float—I can't to this day float. I happen to have a bone marrow structure apparently that doesn't allow floating. In fact, the Negroid race is also predominant in this, although I don't know what kind of background I may have had, but I am white. But in swimming I had a lot of power, and by this time had built up some endurance, but I wasn't getting myself kinda like a bull seal in the water or something like this, I was doing a lot of work and not making it. I can remember at one time thinking I would never do it. Then, of course, I felt that holding your breath in the water, with timing and breathing, was a tremendous challenge. This was because water to me was just not a natural place for the human being to be in this horizontal position. As we would build up and build up, my times were very, very, very, just on the hairline, whether I was going to make the mile in 60 minutes.

The other aspect of our three-weeks pre-training was the rubber boat work. The officers had been given at that time the privilege to have two weeks pertaining to be able to more or less screen them and to make this individual, to give him the opportunity to be a better leader in front of enlisted men. And it did screen out what we called the shit birds, because when we got into training we were totally unmarked. If you came out of the training, we lived as boat crews; we lived in the boats; we slept in the boats. Everywhere you went you were in this boat. The boat is a rubber boat called a

7-man IBS, inflatable boat, small. Normally there would be four enlisted and one officer assigned to this boat. You would carry it on your head, you would carry it in what they called the low carry, hip carry, shoulder carry, through various commands. To bring about the discipline of the group, putting them together, the boat is a very, very effective training method, which tends to organize a small group to work effectively together. We were then given our first assignments. To patch the boat, they gave us a kind of a rubber that had been not too worthy as far as holding air. It took quite a period to bring this boat into what we call seaworthiness, although that was an extremely good test.

I can remember the four men I was given. One was Hans Poppy. He was a German refugee who had grown up in Berlin during WWII. He was 6'4" and weighed about 220 pounds. He still had a little bit of a German accent in his dialect and was strictly of the German character in the perfection and the drive that this race of people tend to exhibit. The other was Bob Hayes, who was kind of a heavy man, 5'10", and was an excellent swimmer. He had a personality that I can't ever remember him getting mad or too disturbed, and always had a consistent pleasant nature about him. Then there was a guy named Lightfoot from Florida. He was probably, at least I considered at that time, the weakest man in my crew. However, his advantage was that he had been in UDT's before but had gotten out. At that time before you could get back in you had to go through training. So, I felt that the experience he could bring, and later proved to be, would be of great assistance to us. Then there was Fuller. Fuller was a very well-built man, 5'10", 190 pounds, and extremely brilliant. He had the highest rating a man can get in his adaptability tests, which in the Navy is, I believe, a score of 72 or 73, and he had a score of 70. He was within two points of the highest you can get. He could take three figures each way. Like you give him 333, 433, 533, and give me an answer, and he'd have it multiplied faster than the computer or a calculator could. But he carried a chip on his shoulder, so he was the other man I thought I would have trouble with.

And, of course, in all events everything that is done in this training is by boat crew. So, it's up to the leader of the boat crew, called a cocksun, to try to hold the group together. This was an important role because any training, any knowledge or anything else that you could get together as a crew would be to your advantage at a later date, which is the big date ahead that we were pointing ourselves to, Hell Week. With this in mind, we continued through our three-week training. I was still able to keep these men together and keep working with them and to continue driving forward. It was characteristic that, although I usually could find a place up in the front, to revert to my position as an officer in the boat.

The importance of leadership was first exhibited while we were on our runs. To be able to although as I say, I had at that time been able to establish that I could run up into the forward areas in the runs. It was characteristically looked upon by the instructor crew to observe your leadership tendencies and characteristics. Naturally, the thing to do would be to circle back and try to bring the members of your boat crew on, to talk to them and see what you could do with them. Although we didn't feel, or have never felt, that UDT or SEAL training was part of babysitting, I think one of the things that this leadership started to develop, and probably is the most important internal function for the success the UDTs and SEALS have ever had, is the buddy system. To care for each other and to learn the mutual respect of each other was part of this system, and I think our training was somewhat the start of its inception. If your leader cared, your instructor cared, it made a better scene all the way around.

But anyway, we started forming up, and had the preliminary boat work and our crews. I can always remember my crew was what I thought of as being big men, and I think if I were to have selected even then and immediately, they were the men assigned to us, but if I were to have selected a crew, I don't think I would have picked too many other individuals other than the ones I had assigned to me. Then again, it was making the best of what you have, which is still an integral part of the UDT-SEAL idea.

CHAPTER V

Hell Week

Then came Hell Week. This is something that really perked us up—we built up if it can be conceived of. But we, on the Saturday before Hell Week, which always started at midnight on Sunday night of the third week, we ran, and this wasn't Hell Week, we ran. 17 miles behind Old Tree Trunk, the horse. In fact, that is the only time I remember seeing a little perspiration drip down his back. If for no other reason, thinking back, of five weeks prior, the earlier runs into in that short of period to build up to a 17-mile run. In fact, it was farther for the individuals in front, because they would circle around with the instructors.

I can remember that my parents came out to see me the Sunday before the Sunday night that we reported in for Hell Week. I could hardly remember anything, and I was so nervous I could not even talk to them. It was kind of somewhat like having the bull by the tail and he's running 90 miles an hour and you can't let loose. It's a helluva predicament to be in. Then we reported in. Everybody had to live in one certain barracks, about midnight. They let you get just kind of about halfway asleep (although you didn't—you had to have both eyes awake) and here they came. Throwing Mark 80 firecrackers and flares and yelling for muster in 5 minutes. You had to be standing tall with your boat and boat crew, and one of the things that was to keep us alive but was a tremendous nuisance, was the peacock life jacket -- this was a big old jacket you always had to suit up and wear. And, naturally, the trainees were dirty. We went out on the weekend and hadn't cleaned ourselves properly, so we'd have to get into the bay and clean off. San Diego Bay was known as a completely filthy bay but it's not, you know. So, we must have been pretty dirty to have to get in there and get cleaned up from our weekend. And from that point on I don't remember being dry for a period by drying with a towel, and perhaps if you had a wife like I did, slipping some of the clothing apparel that she could slip to us somewhere along the line, through this Hell Week. Then, of course, we'd get back to bed maybe two or three in the morning and we would be kind of somewhat cold standing out there. They asked if we were cold, and we said no. It was always necessary to say no, we're warm. An instructor somewhere along the line would always find someone shivering, or claim he did, so we would have to go for a run along the beach. I can remember running along the beach with the surf pounding away during low tide, and the water kind of a shimmered on the sand, a glitter came from the water. The instructors had a jeep behind us going back and forth, which kind of reminded me of what it might be like to be a prisoner. After all this we'd finally get to bed and, naturally, we would forget to clean up our boats. They were dirty also, so we'd have to get back into the bay and clean those off. Then came Monday morning, and it was time to rise and shine and smile and notice the sun coming up and enjoy the new great day.

We always started the day in the normal routine of calisthenics. During that first Hell Week calisthenics were a rather excruciating experience to say the least. They put you to what we called parade rest right at that point, and from that point on everything was more or less competitive. The boat crews would try to build up this group spirit, this internal fraternalism. We would work as boat crews competing against other boat crews. Part of this meant that the first boat crew would get points if that crew was the first to muster, which almost, at all times, was the first boat crew out of the chow hall. I will say, speaking of chow, that this is where we learned an important point, that a man can go quite a lengthy time without sleep, but he's got to have food to burn to create the energy, which we did. We ate, regardless of how horrible it tasted, although it was excellent food, the fatigue and the sore lips and sore throats, etc., lung areas, you'd throw it down, and you'd have to. The more you ate, the better you were. But still, first crew out of the chow hall got points.

Log Training (US Naval Amphibious Base, Coronado, California)
(Source: Personal collection of John Randall Stephenson, Esq.
All rights reserved.)

One thing that I can say about Hell Week is that it is something that will remain with a man once he goes through it, there will never be a time in his life, and I have never experienced, and I feel that I have gone through some extraordinary experiences, and I can never remember there was never a time of difficulty that equaled Hell Week. It's a tremendous confidence program, although it is sometimes hard to make the layman understand, as we would call it in this aspect, or the psychiatrist or whoever would be probing into this individual's mind to understand this program, as I've found out. But after breakfast, of course, we had PT before and after breakfast, we'd go on a nice little run, about two miles, but a good hard run. Then we'd form up into relay races, nuisance races they'd call it. It was various relays, the wheelbarrow, pushing the rock or something across with sand with your nose, or a snake race, or something where you grabbed both of your toes — I'm not too limber of an individual, I think this was, to most, called a duck walk, where we'd grab our toes with our hands, and walk around down to a certain distance and back all in a race. There were several disciplines we'd have to go through to as soon as your boat crew was finished and in line, then the Officer In Charge would have to run over and shout the name. We always would have to carry our paddles with us and carry them in the manner as you would a rifle. Again, a very, very good discipline technique, as I later found out. Then after the nuisance races in the morning, we'd have log PT. This is a 300–500-pound log that we'd have to do various sit-ups with, push-ups on, both in and out of the water, and in the surf. This really formed the boat crew because if one man wasn't carrying his weight, well, the log never got maneuvered in the manner it was directed.

Fellow Officers

At this time, which seemed like the week was already past, I can also remember that we went to lunch, the officers in my crew: Jim Kenny, he'd been a football player from Yale, a fine man; Doug Allred, also a football player, went to the University of Arizona; John Schmidt, later went to medical school and became a physician, and a very close friend; all of these people were close friends; Bill Texido, super salesman from Tufts College; John Schmidt was from California, went to the University of California, Berkeley. We got together, and they were all deciding that this was nonsense for us to compete and draw our energies to get our endurance as low as we were seemingly doing. So, this was the proposed plan. We would let one crew win one time and another crew win another time, and we'd kind of back off. Well, this didn't seem to be part of my makeup. I feel that if you're going to do something you have to drive hard all the way. So, I guess I in some fashion became a turncoat among my contemporaries. I had it in my mind to win Hell Week. By winning Hell Week, we got the last night off. And for the first day it didn't seem like a big thing. But by Wednesday and later in the week it was important. It probably seemed, of course, that looking from the outside we were a bunch of children fighting over nothing. But it became very, very important to have that sleep. Sleep became an extreme figure in your head.

Mudflats

So, after lunch we proceeded with the boats on our heads about four miles down to the mudflats, which are down at the end of the San Diego Bay by the Coronado City Dumps. It's just a horrible, smelly cesspool. (In fact, I have some clothes to this day, which would be some 11 or 12 years later, that still have that smell in them.)

The training at the mudflats was something that I really, really enjoyed. All my life Mom said I couldn't play in the mud. And out here I was playing in the mud. And, of course, it was kind of fun. I remember yelling over to Jim Kenny as we were doing various relay races and other exercises through the mud and asked him what his contemporaries from Yale were doing at this time, and whether he felt he was keeping up with them. I don't feel that he was too happy with my comments. Particularly because they at that time found out I wasn't playing their "be a good guy" games. The purpose of the mud is, as it was explained to us, that several times during the Korean conflict, some of the UDT's had done demolition work and had escaped through the sewers, or, as we called them "shit ditches," that they have in those countries. (I later did the same in capturing individuals in southeast Asia.) After the mudflats, which occurred all afternoon, we got the privilege of paddling back in the bay. Although the wind was against us, they gave us a bonus point for the first crew to get back there to chow.

UDT Trainees at the Coronado Mudflats (1961)
(Source: Personal collection of John Randall Stephenson, Esq. All rights reserved.)

Boat Crews

One of the requirements for the crews was to have our boat maintained in an immaculate manner. During training at the mudflats, we'd been rolling and working in the mud all afternoon. It probably came up to about our waists and it was a very mushy consistency type material. By this time, however, we were starting to pull ahead in points and these guys in the crew started to gel a little bit.

But there were a few holes in the program. There was no way in anyone's mind that we could conceive of coming through on it, but we were attempting to clean up ourselves and our boat in the bay and little did we realize we had our boat cleaned off, we had ourselves cleaned up to an acceptable degree, yet we were standing there in mud or had mud in our shoes. As we began to paddle towards the base to the chow hall, a distance of about 2-1/2 or 3 miles, I noticed that we had pulled mud into the boat and got it dirty. And decided that we'd get the thing clean. I gave the command to hold water, which meant to stop paddling, for all men into the water, and this Fuller, who was my number one paddler and stroke man had said, "Sir, we could go over there," which was part of the way out of the way. I had learned enough about navigation to know that we would be working against the tide to go over on a nice little recreational beach where the sand would be, and quite naturally, his approach made sense. But I did not think his approach had to do with getting between one point to another and using the currents to our best advantage. So, I said, "Fuller, in the water." He turned and said "Sir, I've got more time in the brig than you've got in the Navy." With no other alternative at hand, I reached over with my paddle neatly split it across his head. Didn't make too big a gash in his head and the blood didn't appear to bother him too much.

So, we finally got Fuller and ourselves cleaned up and got going. We were still the second boat and still had a good chance to be the first boat to the base when I started giving a lecture on the officer's commission. I said, "Perhaps you men don't understand the commission and what it signifies, and perhaps you've worked with officers or (remembering the individuals that I had first come in contact with at OCS), that some of the officers you've come in contact with may not have been able to uphold the commission to the extent that is been designed to be." Then I said, "This isn't the case here." About that time Fuller started laughing. And I thought "Uh-oh! This guy's gonna go all the way with me." I said, "Fuller, what's your problem?" and he just smiled and said, "I've never had the commission explained to me in the manner you have just explained it," and he stroked away. He later became one of my best men. We did get to the base first.

At this point I might add that I conceived of an idea for the boat, or it was perhaps passed on to me by Rusty Campbell, when he said, "Don't ever bring it out or expect me to inspect your boat" (because we were inspected at all times for various items of comfort that we might stow away in the boat some way or another by the instructors), but he or I felt that if I put two floor mats in the boat, these are air-inflated floor mats, this would give my boat more stability, although a little heavier, but I had bigger men to be able to carry it. I felt this would be a good idea that was passed on by an instructor, kind of on the QT. At that time, we had a pretty good idea we were probably one of the better boats as far as getting from point A to B in water.

So, the first day, after chow, we were given a briefing on a night problem. The problem was to paddle and portage the boat (portage means to carry the boat on the heads of the crew) throughout various points on the base, in San Diego Bay and around Coronado, including paddling around a rock jetty in front of the Del Coronado Hotel, which was a resort hotel. The rock jetty stuck out in the water where the surf happened to hit the jetty at a very rapid pace. It could be excruciating to maneuver, possibly breaking up the boat, and pressing your body in the rocks and water and at a speed that wasn't normally considered comfortable to say the least. But to master the rock program was simply a matter of timing the surf to get in there and get your crew and paddle and work together, because if you didn't work together the breaker was going to get you. Maneuvering the rock jetty probably took until about midnight or somewhere past that point. Then, somewhere along the line, we would be brought in to have our fourth meal of the day. There were always check points that you had to go by to report in. Of course, the winning boat crew for the night problem received a great number of points in line with the competition. After this we were given the opportunity to go to bed.

There again, which you get just nice and warm and cozy and drift off into just about what would be near sleep, deep sleep, then you would hear the usual "muster in five minutes." These periods were called "break-outs." During a break-out, you'd go out, and naturally were told somebody had fouled up. The instructors were working on you, they were trying to get you. Right here is the point where most men quit. If you can get past this part, you've got the better part of it made. We would work to get all our men out, that was it. But then, there was always somewhere along the line somebody goofed up, and we had to correct this. He didn't stack his boat in the right manner. This was to try to supposedly tear down our images of class, even though we were working as a boat crew, we still maintained spirit. Without singing the song that we sang, about the thought of being a tiger, the strongest individual, we would not have had the mental drive to make it. There was no way possible that I know. So, these breakouts would occur again two or three times a night. Probably the most you could get would be 45 minutes of sleep. And then to be somewhere in a position of heading towards bed again as the sun came up and calisthenics would begin again.

Swimming Pool Training

The second day was similar to the first day, except that in place of the mudflats in the afternoon we went to the swimming pool. While in the swimming pool we had relay races. During these relay races was where Hayes came through, our swimmer. The point of all these things was to design a way to work as a crew. Ingenuity was just the only way I can put it. The quicker you can work together; this is where you can learn to work and to think when you're at what you consider a disadvantage. Relay races, such as swimming a 40-pound weight across the pool, or swimming two cigarette papers across the pool without getting them wet, and all types of things. One was king of the boat, which was introduced later, kind of relieved some of the built-up tensions which might be occurring throughout the training period. I can remember in one of three pool periods, Fuller was always like myself, prone to cold a little more than the average man. We apparently had some kind of thin skin. He got cold one afternoon and was going to quit. So, I instructed Poppy to place his head underwater to the extent that when he shook his head no, he wasn't going to quit, this was a matter of making what was difficult to him seem more difficult, so therefore being on the side of the pool with the wind whipping around you was not as bad as being in the water in a lengthy period without any source of air. The week pretty much continued alternating on Thursday. But I will say by Tuesday morning after the breaks, half of the class was gone in an average situation. Then they'd always say that if you got past Tuesday morning, that's when most of the people would drop out. This was totally a volunteer program; you could drop out at any time.

CHAPTER VI

Hell Week Continues

At one point on Wednesday night, we were allowed to sit behind a sand dune and rest. This gave us some mental anguish. We just more or less walked around, and they asked us how we were. It's quite a feeling to wonder what was up, what the problem was, why we were getting this little extra consideration. Never did find out. It was rather nice; however, you couldn't enjoy it because you were sitting there wondering what was going to happen next, plus, just by sitting there for a period while you weren't active, you got quite cold and would begin to shiver. By Wednesday evening our boat crew had built up a sizable lead in the competition. Still, we had not lost a man, which is very unusual. In fact, I later finished with the same four men that I started with, and this is supposedly, was claimed to be, the first boat crew in the history of UDT training to have the same individuals start and finish.

Wednesday night we started to slip a little, I noticed, a little bit of arguing, bickering, a few things weren't happening, and we did have one boat crew who was pushing us. This crew was rather strange. It was run by a cocksun named Schultz, whom I have not brought up yet. Dale Schultz was from Iowa. He was about one of the toughest officers with more mental desire and was, I felt, the best runner we had in the class, a pretty good swimmer, and just all-around physically very strong. However, from the common-sense standpoint and leadership, very weak. He'd been to seminary school and theological schools, and was strong in this background, but from just the day to day living and knocks on the road, he hadn't had too much of yet. Schultz's boat crew was made up of four smaller, but extremely strong and tough men. I remember there was Joe Messinger. We called him Little Joe. He's still in the UDT's. And a little guy named Byrd.

UDT Trainees During Hell Week (1961)
(Source: Personal collection of John Randall Stephenson, Esq.
All rights reserved.)

A UDT Trainee Enjoying Hell Week (1961)
(Source: Personal collection of John Randall Stephenson, Esq.
All rights reserved.)

Byrd was the toughest man I'd ever run into in my life. In fact, I remember one time we had worked our way up after the run started. People started falling out and this was the first three weeks of training. People started falling out of number one position, and I edged up forward. However, Jim Kenny likewise did the same, and we kind of met at the same time looking at each other. But Jim, being the courteous individual that he was, turned to me and said "take it," and I said "No, you take it." In the meantime, Byrd slips in and says "Oh well, I'll do it," and, naturally, I couldn't see this happening. This wasn't quite the idea that Kenny and I had in mind. So, I went over and gave him a tremendous elbow and shoulder and knocked him out of the position. In fact, knocked him over about three feet into the berm. He just got up, just bounced up and says, "Oh well, I guess I won't take it." Byrd got the last word, however. I can remember later in the run, Tree Trunk opened up and naturally, I didn't know where he was going or where he was going to stop, but he really kind of started to leave me. Then I can remember starting to fall back a little bit. Tree Trunk was still moving out. I think Schultz was the only other individual ahead of me. All of a sudden, I could hear footsteps running behind me, coming up faster and faster. I happened to look back and there was Byrd, and he was moving out. I decided that I wasn't going to let him pass me. I kept running and running and running, harder until finally I just could not go anymore, or thought I could not. Anyway, I started falling back. Byrd came by and patted me on the butt and said, "Come on, sir. Don't give up. Let's go! Let's don't quit." I was never so mad in my life. If I could have gotten my hands on that guy. I don't know what I would have done.

Anyway, back to Wednesday night. We were kind of edgy, and this other boat crew, Schultz's boat crew, was starting to get to us. I think it looked like they were going to, actually, they always could out-portage us, but we needed to try to get ahead of them by paddling, and this happened to be one night it looked like they were going to beat us at paddling. So, I told them that if we beat that Schultz's crew to our next checkpoint, that I would buy them a steak dinner at the Mexican Village, which took care of it. The men started pulling together, and we won the paddling that night.

CHAPTER VII

Mexican Village

The Mexican Village is a very well-known bar and restaurant in Coronado, California. It is a place that people go to meet each other, particularly male and female. Although the fella's got practically every group of people that would be in an area like, something for them in his restaurant. Sunday morning, he takes care of the church crowd with a brunch, and in the evening, he had tremendous meals, and after that's the jet set or the night set where he has a nice little band, and all the young Naval officers and older ones, come in to enjoy themselves.

My first experience in the Mexican Village was when I was still on the ship. We had come into San Diego, and I had gone out on the beach with some of my friends from the ship. It was late at night. We had been drinking somewhat through the evening. I was, being on ensign's pay, out of money. So, we happened to end up in the Mexican Village, where I remember ordering, not having much money, I believe, 12 tortillas. The reason for this is that I had noticed some pilots sitting in a booth—the booths were kind of made of palm leaves, etc., with each area being individual—but a booth across from us where some young pilots were talking about their flying experiences and they were flying planes using their hands as illustrations of various positions, etc. I don't know what it was. So, I thought it was rather appropriate to purchase these tortillas and engage in a flying fest with these men. When my tortillas came, they were nice and hot. Steaming. Sailed very well. I remember sailing a couple, throwing them like a disk down the aisle. So, therefore, I started throwing these tortillas, making various sounds which should near resemble an airplane. I think they looked rather surprised as these tortillas slapped them in the face. However, we got into one of the first fights that I'd gotten into in Mexican Village, and that was the start of the long association with the management and the owner of the Village.

Another time, about three years later, I can recall being out with Dave Bramble. Dave was a huge, approximately 250-pound football player from Stanford, a very photogenic individual. He and I were at that time instructors together, and we were out for the evening. I can recall going in the Mexican Village after one of our drinking fests that had occurred somewhere or another. We entered the Mexican Village wearing swim trunks, where coat and tie was required. Dave was behind me hollering, "Clear out—the Frogs are here." By this time, most people either tolerated or ignored us. However, there was an Air Force Colonel who did not heed my word or listen to me and I can remember going up to him and saying, "Hey Buddy, did you hear what we said?" And he said, "I don't move out for anyone at any time." I remember taking his hat, putting it on my head, picking him up and sliding him down the bar. Of course, again, I was escorted out and asked not to come back; this time getting a formal letter from the Sheriff.

Anyway, back to Hell Week. The agreement to give them a steak dinner at the Mexican Village was effective, and we did win the race that night. Thursday was, of course, a day when we were really punchy, a day when you are just about psychologically disoriented and depleted. However, it was the same kind of day as any other during Hell Week except for the fact we, I believe, went to the swimming pool in the morning, and back to the mudflats in the afternoon.

Thursday evening, however, was quite an evening. This is the night where you carried the boat on your head 25 miles. This is the night when they talked about blood in your boots. This is where it comes, this is where by Friday, every piece of living matter in your body is sore and tired and disoriented and disarrayed. But all week, as I had stated before, we had been given a briefing on a night problem, given checkpoints, given areas to go, and told how to do it.

On Thursday night it's called a treasure hunt. You were not allowed to paddle, but they did not brief you other than the rules as to what you could or could not do. Which meant, you couldn't carry your boats on vehicles. You couldn't do various methods to short circuit the program, other than carrying your boat on your head. But, to get from one point to another, the problem was given to you in the form of a riddle. This approach was very, very challenging and rewarding in my mind to have been able to have been as tired and far gone as we were, to sit down and figure the whole program, as to where you would go and what you would do at that stage in the game using those riddles. Because, believe me, they were hard. I later thought, years later, when I was an instructor, that maybe it was just hard to us then, but looking at various other riddles that we made up for trainees in classes, that they were just hard. We went throughout the evening, the first part of the evening it seemed like the instructor, by this time we had Murphy, he somehow liked us and got to liking me for some reason or another. I don't know why. I remember he brought us a 6-pack of beer by that evening, and we felt he was the greatest friend in the world. Most of our riddles were ones where the solutions took us to points in the area mostly around the base and an area that didn't take us too far. (Of course, again, you'd still have hopes that the whole evening was going to be a nice evening, and that all you'd heard about Thursday night was a hoax to keep your pucker factor up.) At midnight we were given a riddle which directed us to go to the chow hall, which was rather easy to figure out. I had previously noticed that all boat crews hit the chow hall at the same time. So, I told my crew that we had to eat in a hurry and get out because I felt that the first boat crew out of the chow hall had a better chance of winning the evening and, if we were to win Thursday night, our lead would have been substantial enough to make it impossible not to win and get off Friday night.

Murphy was nice enough to give our riddle to us before we sat down to chow and we had it figured out before we were done. The riddle was "Big, black, and bad," and we figured it was the rocks in front of the Hotel Del Coronado. As we were leaving the chow hall, Poppy, who by this time was a big elephant, seemingly running out of gas, came up and asked me if he could go to the head, which was across the street from the chow hall in the enlisted man's barracks. I told him he could and to meet us at a stop light located outside the base crossing the highway going down to the beach, and from there on up the beach about a mile or so to the rock, and we told him we'd meet him at this stoplight out on the highway, of course. Well, we got out to the stoplight, and we set the boat down. We did not think too much about it, other than a time period building up, but then we noticed a first boat crew starting to approach us. Then from there we noticed that Murphy started giving us what we call lip or smoke and asked whether we were having problems.

Right then I can remember seeing our lead and everything else crumble as the boat crews came by us, giving us a tremendous amount of encouragement, or whatever they wanted to do. Here we were, the top boat crew, which was no longer on top because we were shy a man. We were just sitting there. The other crews didn't know, of course, whether one of us had quit or just what our problem was. But I can remember it seemed kind of like a quarterback in football when the other team has turned the momentum on the quarterback and things are going a little difficult. It is at those times that you find out what you can and cannot do. So, I ran back, assuming or thinking that Poppy had probably gone to sleep, or something of this nature. I remember thinking that, by the way Murphy was giving me some comments and his statements, that he may have gone and hidden Poppy somewhere. (I'd heard that once you get in the lead so far, the instructors tend to try to even it up.) I ran approximately 3/4's of a mile back to the area of the head that Poppy was in. Sure enough, I ran in this one, I don't know why, there were several, but I ran in this one particular one, and there he was sound asleep. I was so infuriated that I backhanded him as hard as I could and bloodied his mouth and nose. He started running with his pants down and his lifejacket on. I can remember looking in the stool and he hadn't done anything, so I was sure his intentions were good. He was just a big man who had run out of gas. All the way back I ran behind Poppy, just nipping and giving the lecture that I didn't care about me or him. I let him know that he'd let the other men in his crew down, and if we didn't win this tonight, then we could just about count on a very, very tight date on Friday, and that this wasn't according to our game plan.

All this time he was just hollering, "I'm sorry, Mr. Stephenson, I'm sorry," and he was just quite naturally, crying like a baby. So, we got out to the boat, and all the boat crews had passed us by this time. Fuller was fit to be tied. Then Poppy got under the boat. Normally, it takes four men to carry the boat with one man carrying the paddles, but Poppy took off running carrying the boat himself. I told him to go down the highway even though we weren't supposed to go down the highway, which paralleled the beach to the hotel, so that we would be able to have a harder surface to run on. This was somewhat of a shortcut. The reason for not being able to run on the highway is that the men that are wet, in green clothing and a black boat on a black highway are nearly impossible to be observed. Anyway, we ran down the highway, and Poppy all the way saying, "I'm sorry, guys. I'm sorry." He literally carried the boat at almost a dead run for the entire two-mile distance. It was all we could do, I know I switched the paddles once to someone else on the way down, just to keep up with him. It turned out we ended being the number two boat crew at the hotel at the rock jetty.

At that point we received a riddle which said, "keep the birds in," which meant to go to the North Island Air Station fence. This was about another two miles away from the base. So Poppy was still wound up, and we were the first boat crew to get to the fence at North Island. However, after we got there, we were given a riddle which said, "try the other one on for size," which meant a fence at the state park which was six miles in the opposite direction. At this time, I can remember telling one of the instructors, Klondike Ike, who continued to laugh, that it was a good thing they put this in on Thursday night, or I would quit right then and there. So, we sat around on our boats for a little bit, bitching, etc., and finally decided to take off. Through this little period of lull, Schultz's crew caught up with us and passed us. It looked like Schultz's crew was going to pull away from us as we were heading back toward the rock jetty from the North Island fence. But by then I finally I had a plan figured out that I thought might work. So, I told the men that if they would give a strong effort and pass up that crew by the time we got to the rocks or before then, I could practically guarantee them that we would stay away from them. I was going to go talk to their boat coxswain. So, I went up to Schultz and he said "Oh, my goodness, yes." So, I said, "Schultz, this is rather ridiculous that you and I are so far ahead of the other boat crews, that we should have time to rest somewhere along the line then get ahead of them again," because we felt we had the ability to get ahead. He agreed.

So, I said, "Well,"—his name was Dale—Dale, when we come to the rocks up here, I'm so far ahead of your boat, and it's just about the distance of the width of this rock jetty, so when we get there we'll go on over to the other side and then you position someone, when you see us, go on down the beach, this means that we've just gone on and taken off, and then that way we can get back to our race."

So, as we crossed the rock jetty, I noticed that Schultz's boat and men had stopped, and I just told my men to walk easy. We didn't see Schultz's men for the rest of the night. I felt this was kind of a sadistic way to win a set of completion, however, at that stage of the game, it appeared that ethics were not really that important (as we'll find out later in this work that we've been involved in the past few years).

After all of this we went on into Friday, as I say. We were extremely sore and tired. I could remember one time as an instructor I had a friend from Wyoming. I had him convinced to go in the Navy, much the same as I. He never had any experience with the Navy or water, and, was a not too good of a runner—it turned out he was a better water man than a runner. His name was Gary Lanphier. This is when I was an instructor. My sister, MaryAnn Stephenson, had come out to see me from Wyoming and she had gone through 12 years of school with Gary. I was in the office and my sister was sitting in the car along with my wife outside the office, when Gary sneaks up around the outside of the car to talk to my sister. My sister asked him how the training went and what it was like. Gary said, "Well, you can see movies on it, you can read books on it, they can tell you all about it, you talk about it, but until there's blood in your boots, you never know what it's like."

Anyway, Friday morning was the very, very high point of fatigue, but we had enough points so that is what we were holding on to that for the day. This became our reason for existing, our reason for continuing. However, and we did know that this was going to happen, they would be taking points away from us for everything possible. We felt that we would still be the first boat crew off, but never would we know until it actually happened, or when it would occur. And we went through Friday morning in this manner.

Demolition Harassment

Friday afternoon was what we called Demolition Harassment. This was where we would crawl through or near demolition explosives, half pound and pound blocks of TNT (Trinitrotolvene) and HBX (High Blast Explosive) going off, shooting live rounds above us, and crawling under barbed wire aprons. I can remember, naturally, trying to win the boat crew and exhibit the leadership that we felt we were supposed to have, volunteering to be the first man to run into the demolition course. On the way down the course, I couldn't believe it, they started setting off a charge just exactly at the point where they told me I was to jump to and climb under. The first one didn't bother me but the second one did. And one went off, I'm sure, within two steps of my having to take a leap for this area and having to crawl under the fence. It was a very, very stimulating experience to have these charges going off almost within arms distance of your body. Naturally, it was very highly controlled by the instructors, and they had vision of all shots and control of all shots before they occurred. However, it was a real experience for one who has never been through it. Friday, the rest of the evening, just went along just like normal, and we were given a briefing to continue a night problem and start out on it, go through the night problem. By this time the guys, we were just almost to the point of not caring, we made sure that we had our boats adequately stocked with wine and honey and graham crackers and what not. I remember our first checkpoint, when they called my boat crew, I believe it was Boat Crew 4, and told us to get leaning rest and do pushups. They kept having us do pushups and pushups. Little did I know why.

It was an instructor, Ron Smith, who said finally, "Okay, take your boat back to the base and secure. You've won Hell Week."

We were so excited we ran around like little kids, running into each other, and running over everything, naturally. My only intent that I can remember at that time was to get those guys in that boat and get out of there before that damned instructor changed his mind. After we got ourselves secured, we went to the chow hall and ate. Then, you would not believe it, but we did not go home, we did not go to bed, we instead hustled off at that time to the local hangout in Coronado called the Island for a few brews before going home. After getting home and arriving there, of course, early, we were, of course fortunate, but it seems as though a man could sleep about 18 hours, wake up for 30 minutes, and then sleep for another 18 hours.

By Monday, however, we were ready to go back to training. Now this was still the following Monday. It was still one of the biggest hurdles. Training—all the training was one hurdle after another—you crossed one hurdle and you had another. This came to be the pattern that was established with this program.

Mile Swim

As part of our training, I still had to make a one-mile swim in 60 minutes, and we had swum up to about 3/4 of a mile before Hell Week. But we had to make some ocean swims starting at a half mile, working up to 3/4 mile, then back to the pool for the timed mile. Any trainee who didn't make this timed mile was automatically dropped from training. This was an awful time to be dropped after going through and putting out the efforts that you had in Hell Week. When we make this mile, it's marked in a swimming pool with buoys at four corners, and you swim around each buoy.

This is all okay if an individual is in the water by himself. However, this was not the case. They put whatever number of men were left in our training class, I think we had 35 men or something like that at that time, and everybody gets in the water and starts swimming.

It also happened to be the first day we had a small indoctrination lecture on the face mask, which was the first time we were given face masks. So, the face mask was a problem to have to overcome.

I can recall being naturally psyched up for this swim. But, having this face mask on my face, I got a little claustrophobic with that darn thing on. Several times I wanted to reach up and rip it off and throw it at one of the instructors. Then there was one point where some of the better swimmers had finished, and I was still going along. I had the feeling that I was over my time, and was convinced of it because of the face mask, that I came over to the side of the pool and remember seeing H. O. Cunningham saying, "Relax, relax, this is going to be your new home, you've got to relax more in the water." I knew right then and there I was through, and then he'd keep walking along the side of the pool just giving me, "Come on, you can make it, come on." All I could do if I knew he cared was just to smile and move out. Lo and behold, when I got out of the water, my time was 59 minutes and 30 seconds. I had it made.

CHAPTER VIII

Post Hell Week

Then we were given another test. We had to do a mile in the ocean. I might say at this time that a Frogman has always been noted for wearing a black wetsuit, but up until this time in training we did not have anything representing a wetsuit, and we were only given a wetsuit top along with the issuance of our fins, which meant the completion of our mile in 60 minutes, plus a mile in the ocean. And then, this thing would have been best not to have had it given to us, because it became a threat because we were always worried about whether we were going to get to wear our wetsuits when it would have been better off not to even have had to worry about the damned things. But when we were given fins, for some reason or another, because of my legs and football background, whatever it might be, I came from being the last timed swimmer in the class to number three or four, and that is where I remained as my position or class standing in swimming the rest of the class. It somehow worked well for me. But I could remember, Doug Allred, was doing very well in swimming, but he was a big fella, a big lineman, football types were never good runners out on the beach, but most of them were pretty good swimmers. And this was Doug's only claim to fame, and I seemed to have most of the things going for me that everybody else seemed to want. Doug was having problems being called in and getting warnings and reprimands and so on and so forth from the instructing staff, but he still had one thing going for him, was his swimming. But for some reason or another when he got the fins, he couldn't move the things for beans. And I can remember passing him up and he flew me the bird—it really got to him to see me pass him up in the fins. However, later, he mastered the fins.

Now we could swim, we had been screened and we had proven we could withstand Hell Week. Now it was time to get about the business of UDT and what it was about. Naturally, we had gone through two weeks of pre-training, and then, of course, four weeks, including Hell Week, of pre-training, and now we had a remainder of 12 weeks to finish. This is where we got actual training in diving, demolition, reconnaissance and combat tactics, and the expertise that goes into this type of background. (I won't go into the actual details of various situations as I have my notes which I took while in training, and several lesson plans that can be derived for backgrounding, so I'll just try to departmentalize it in a quick brief rundown and go from there.) Naturally, the reconnaissance phase taught us charting, the making of beaches from the 3-fathom foot mark on water, into the high-water line, and through what we called the firm and hinter land.

The point of this phase of it was to select or find obstacles and mines, chart beach gradient so that a selection of the proper type landing craft or landing ship could be made, and the length of time they could remain on the beach to allow floats, supplies, troops, whatever else the case may be. Then there was the demolition phase, where we went through and learned about all types of military explosives, the characteristics of military explosives, and the understanding, use, safety precautions, and how to best apply them in charts, calculations, etc. We were given a phase in land combat tactics, which consisted of training in stealth, concealment, weapons, and use of weapons—very, very basic. We also learned scouting, patrolling, sentry stalking and hand to hand combat, all of which was very introductory and basic. Then we had the diving phase, where we were given an aqua lung or open circuit only, and we received a very, very good background in diving physiology and diving timetables, and this sort of thing. In the diving phase there was, of course, a drop in and pickup from the PR.

I might explain about the PR. This is a 40-foot landing craft which is called a personnel recovery boat. It has a little ramp in the front of it. It's a good boat to work on the beach. Over the years we've been given various boats to work with, everything from the fastest jet engine, turbine driven fiberglass boats to small rubber boats. We've been given almost every type that one can imagine. And, out of all this, it is always the old PR that has become our standby. This is the boat that one sees in the movies, where the drop and the pickup in the pictures were. The PR became our secondary lifeline short of the rubber boat.

Free Diving

I can remember one time in the earlier phases of training or our first diving introduction that we had to free dive as we called it. This is diving without any apparatus, to a diving bell about 40 feet down under the water. One of the more difficult portions of free diving was to equalize your eardrums while you are swimming down. Some people can equalize by swallowing, and others must hold their nose and blow. I happened to be one of those individuals at that time.

The purpose of free diving was to get into the bell and do what we called the blow and go, which was to teach us to exhale on the return trip at all times. Free diving gave us the experience of doing this, because anytime air has been taken into the lungs at a compressed rate, in coming to the surface the lungs tend to expand and cause what we call an embolism. If you embolize, you're dead—that's it. So, this was a period of training to be able to comprehend the requirement of having to exhale continually, which is not natural underwater. To continue to exhale, exhale, exhale all the way up to the surface of the water.

I can remember on the way down I was so intent on getting there, or as we called ourselves being a tiger, that I broke my eardrum for the first time. I remember getting a little dizzy and getting into the chamber. The diving bell seemed like it was upside down. But I wouldn't tell them at the time. I went ahead and finished my exercise, but that afternoon, Boy! Did it hurt! This kind of inhibited my diving until the later phases of training. I was allowed to go ahead and go on with everything. It was a matter of just staying out of water for two or three weeks, which was very difficult for me to do. Anyway, we went ahead and finished this learning phase of training. We continued to swim many miles, run many miles, do hours and hours of calisthenics, do many hours of studying after training periods and studying and working with your boat crew—just all in all a very interesting and very intriguing time of one's life.

The last three weeks was the final phase of training which was what we would call the practical aspect—the area where you made it or you didn't. It's not like most schools or something like this where you go through and write a test, pass it, and go out into the world. In UDT training you had to pass satisfactorily and complete every phase of the training. You could not be a specialist in this—not like the Special Forces—where they have a specialist here and a specialist there. (Although they have since learned they must cross-train in all their specialties.) But in UDT training, you had to pass every phase of it. Also, if you wanted to get through, every instructor had to pass you. If there was one instructor who did not want you in the program then you were gone. At the same time, it took all twelve of them to finally come around to telling you that you had to go. This is an area, this mid-phase of training, where most of the fellas were dropped, involuntarily, very involuntarily. Very few of them quit at this point. But I would say at this point they got rid of another 10 to 15 percent of the trainees.

CHAPTER IX

San Clemente Island

After this, those of us remaining went on to the last three weeks of training on San Clemente Island. We went out on a ship, and all the food that was taken out with us. The enlisted trainees had C rations, and the officers were allowed to bring their own canned goods. In fact, I will never eat any more Dinty Moore stew. We took Dinty Moore stew and ate it until it ran out our ears. But this phase of training actually is the practical aspect of it, and this is where we would go out and see if we could apply what we had been given in the classroom and in our lab work. Out there was one of the biggest, most critical times for the officers. This is where they had to again, come back in and exhibit their leadership qualities because the officer was given all the briefings and the problems and he was starting to be given the collar, which he would have within the next few weeks after he became a Team man, or as we would say, gotten the Teams.

John Randall Stephenson, Esq.

San Clemente Island (1961)
*(Source: Personal collection of John Randall Stephenson, Esq.
All rights reserved.)*

Plywood Huts on San Clemente Island (1961)
*(Source: Personal collection of John Randall Stephenson, Esq.
All rights reserved.)*

I will say, I cannot think of or have had any experience where a junior officer in the military can get any more responsibility than they do as a platoon officer or as an Officer In Charge in the UDT's. They are given responsibility immediately upon arrival in the Teams, and they may have a detachment going somewhere in the far parts of the world where they have to work with senior officers, senior people as far as the civilian world is concerned, and perform, in a very, very outstanding manner and do it correctly. But, anyway, we're off to San Clemente Island, to live in tents and sleeping bags. Again, this gets back to Hell Week all over again, except we're doing it under very realistic and practical conditions. I remember on the way out on this LST, and the officer instructors, of course, were living up in the officer country, and the enlisted instructors were living in a forward troops compartment, and the trainee officers were sleeping just aft. This was about a 60-mile trip; however, it was arranged to go on an overnight basis. And I can recall it being in the middle of the afternoon, everything was kind of tidied up and people were around getting rested up, and I was my usual nervous self, worrying about what was coming off, if I was ready or not. I knew the instructors forward of us were asleep, and I had put a bottle of vodka in the arm of my wetsuit prior to departing. Naturally, the alcohol was not allowed on the ship or during training or out in the San Clemente Island. So I thought this would be a good place to hide this item, and, as it turned out, I had forgotten I had put it in there, and I got my wetsuit out to hang it up, and I went through and rechecked my gear.

In UDT your equipment and the maintenance of your gear is a legend. You live with everything being in top operating condition at all times, regardless of what it is. If you think about it, something as minor as breaking the strap on a face mask or being unable to get a knife out of the sheath, could mean your life. It can mean the success or failure of a mission. And this type of detail is very well indoctrinated in your training program.

John Randall Stephenson, Esq.

So, I was going over last-minute check of my gear, and out came this bottle that I had forgotten was in there, spilled all over the deck of the compartment. As soon as the smell of the vodka hit, the instructor for us, Rusty Campbell, came in and called me the dumbest four-letter word that you could ever imagine. He read me up one side and down the other. He proceeded to make me go get a dustpan and pick out the glass first and sweep up this vodka, as much as I could save, and strain it into a jar, which I deposited in his tent upon arrival in San Clemente Island. He continued thereafter to give me a little extra duties here and there and so on and so forth, which I was more than thankful that he did, rather than report it to the authorities.

One of the most difficult and best training situations on San Clemente Island was obstacle loading. These were ton and ton and a half, cement trapezoid and tetrahedron looking obstacles with metal barriers sticking out from them designed to inhibit the passage of boats or small craft through an area. These were used rather heavily in WWII both in the European and Pacific areas, and they would probably not ever be used again, at any time to my knowledge. I would think that mines would be the substitute for these obstacles.

However, I suppose there could be a country that is a poor country that could not afford sophisticated mines, and these obstacles are very economical units to make and can be placed by anyone at any one time. But they would place these obstacles, they would normally supposedly be placed in areas where they could come in contact with boats. However, it was quite characteristic to put some in the surf zone which would be naturally a place where this would be selected as a natural location. Then others were placed up to sometimes 20 to 25 feet deep. These were the ones that brought us to our knees. We would load these with satchel charges, the demolition packs, and blow them later in the training phase. You would have to free dive, there was no air, no wetsuits, and you would spend two or three hours out in the water on these problems, loading these charges, skin-diving, as we called it, free diving down, tying these things on. Then the instructors would come down and put their entire feet and weight and anything else they could do, and if there was absolutely any movement whatsoever of the satchel charge on the obstacle you had to cut it off and do it again. This got a lot of trainees.

I can remember one time we had this colored instructor, Richard Allen. In fact, I can remember when he first came back, he wasn't around our first part of training and through Hell Week. He showed up just after Hell Week. He was a very, very good-looking black man, extremely sharp, and very adaptable, and just an all-around top man. He was the All-Service Boxer, he was the National Golden Gloves Champion, light heavy-weight, and he had been to an all-Navy boxing tournament back east. The first day he arrived and assumed his instructing duties, I guess he somehow selected me and gave me a bunch of extra work to do and ended up making me mad, and I got so mad. I told him I was going to punch him out and to come on over and let's get at it. Had I done this, however, it would have been disastrous, because there would have been no way in the world to handle myself with this man, because I later watched him work in the ring. Every time I think about challenging this individual, I get scared and get butterflies just to think how close I had come. Naturally, he was above it, and he knew what he was trying to do, and I hope not to have met my challenge. However, I can recall when doing our first obstacle loading phases that I had Lightfoot as my loading partner.

The first day we did not do the obstacle loading well at all. It was an unsatisfactory performance, and Allen had mentioned that if you didn't like the job of your partner, or if you couldn't work with him or something like this, to let him know. I think it was just kind of a way for them to find out who they thought was and wasn't doing it. I remember going to him and telling him that I thought my partner had not performed. And I, no sooner said this that I felt like a big ass, because, there again, was a point in life where it's kind of like a football game—you can sit back and say, "Well, we're losing the game, so and so is not playing." But you have to get in and do it. Nobody's going to get you to heaven and nobody's going to get you through this training but yourself. So, you had better get with it. So that is where I turned around and started in.

This was when Old Klondike Ike gave us the deep obstacle. And I can remember tying this thing and tying it well. There was never a time in my life that I felt I had reached such an accomplishment. I could have been designated All American football player or Heisman Trophy winner, and I don't think I would have experienced the joy and satisfaction I did that day when we tied this obstacle at over 25 feet. Actually, one has to realize that it takes about an average of about a minute and a half to get a working dive out of one of these obstacles, and the maximum dive that is taken is up to three minutes. Almost anyone after they finish this UDT training can hold their breath and work underwater for a period of three minutes.

I can remember several times seeing seals coming around, curious, watching us, that didn't stay down as long as we did most of the time. Of course, they did not have any fish to catch, I guess, but their normal dive would seemingly, from what I could observe, last about a minute. Also, one must realize too, that you're in the water up to 2, 2-1/2, 3 hours, sometimes without any protective gear, wetsuit, etc., just your fins, face mask, web belt, and knife. You become extremely cold, and yet you still have to work, and to think and continue to return to an unnatural environment. Looking down at the obstacle, it's very small down there, and nice shadows, and darker looking water between your position and the obstacle on the bottom.

Another time that I thought was rather exciting, through this San Clemente phase, was an exercise called Chase Off Beach. Of course, at that time, we didn't realize that it was called Chase Off Beach. We were briefed and given a briefing, naturally, one of our trainee officers had the problem. This was very interesting, how men who do not know each other, or have never had any background in any way, end up helping each other. We would all pitch in. One would cook, one would clean; we had to cook our own meals. There were no showers. There were no conveniences whatsoever. We cooked on a little two-burner Coleman stove. But, anyway, we were to have a reconnaissance—a night reconnaissance—out of boats, which required a beach party to go in and set up the beach.

CHAPTER X

UDT Training Continued

After the beach party went ashore, it seems like the whole side of the mountain came undone, as there were several charges placed along the rock ledge behind the receiver to be working on that night. And then they started with demolitions and flares and Bouncing Betties (a type of land mine) and then, after we all got to the return and were trying to get out of there, they were actually plunking live rounds down at us. This became a new experience. This is the first time that I had experienced someone shooting at me.

After many years, I can now see the validity of this type of training—at that time I thought it was totally senseless. My first reaction was that of anger, possibly fear, various other attitudes along this particular thing. What you wanted to do was get out of the boat, go back in and settle the score with those people. This, again, is just like when you receive your first rounds in combat, you have an anger program to overcome, you must continue to work rationally, and if not, you may find yourself on the wrong end of the yoyo. People may want you where you think you want to go to get them, and you may not want to be there. So, Chase Off Beach was a valuable experience. It was something that was discussed and talked about for the rest of our training period and years afterwards.

Kelp Swim

One of the more memorable times of the final training phase was a kelp swim. We were given a briefing where we would have to swim a mile through the kelp with boondockers on, or field shoes and no fins. By this time the fins and my original swimming abilities had become quite known throughout the class and instructor force. Before the kelp swim Kevin Murphy gave a lecture which was very convincing, good lecture, good presentation, and he really, really put it on—he put on the dog like nobody could believe. When we got done with that briefing, we knew we were going on one of the toughest swims that man or beast had ever heard, unless you were a seal or a moray eel. We had time to go back to our tents and prepare for the evening kelp swim, and full clothing, no boondocks, in the kelp without fins. I was very, very disturbed and, of course, all of my fellow trainee officers gave me a very bad time. But all of a sudden, they started to think about it themselves a little bit and could see where they thought it wasn't going to be easy also. Again, I remembered thinking of prison and the fact that if we were in prison you were shut up and you were not afforded all the luxuries of life. We were not there, but they were not going to ask you to kill yourself in prison, and this is just what I felt we were getting ready to do.

So, we go on down and muster at the beach and everybody's getting ready to go in. We were to follow the rubber boat full of instructors with a light on it. Then the instructors came up to various trainees and asked them if they wanted to go on the swim.

They said "yes."

Finally, Murphy starts asking more trainees, "Do you want to go on this swim?"

"Yes!" everybody's just shouting.

"Yes, we want to! Yes, we want to go!"

And, at that instance, your mind had been made in such a frame that you were going to do this regardless of what the consequences may be. It was a real psychological effort in this manner. They get you to go in that water through that kelp, which is extremely thick. Although we were told, and kelp will do this, that you can lay on kelp to support your life, but I wasn't going to rely on that too much.

Finally, Murphy said, "Does anybody not want to go?"

There was nobody who did not want to go.

Finally, he said, "Well, let's see."

He came up and asked me and I said "Yes, I want to go".

But he then turned and said, "Mr. Stephenson doesn't want to go, so he doesn't have to go. Fall out!"

He said because of this the night problem had been called off. Of course, there was a period of "Oh gosh, we wanted to go," but I was sure glad we never did the kelp swim.

There was always a place or location where we went to and from the problems we were assigned on San Clemente Island. We had to paddle our rubber boats, again, to all working areas, demolitions areas, hand to hand combat areas and reconnaissance areas, before we would commence the problem. On one exercise, we had to paddle through a place called "the Slaughters". It was a very narrow area at the end of the Island down near China Point. It probably wasn't more than 25 or 30 feet wide, and the surf was very, almost consistently, almost from 5 to 10 feet going through there. Our boat crew always seemed to be fortunate in the surf. However, on one night we got a bad breaker, and it literally threw us and the boat right up on the beach and on the rocks. It tore up the boat and tore us up a little bit with a few scars and stitches. But I can remember Fuller becoming rather disturbed because we had done this, and we finally, at a later date, caught so much havoc from the other boat crews that it was necessary to go into a fisticuff one night back in Coronado behind the Island Bar.

The second time that we were fired on was during a day problem. That time we were on a patrolling problem, and our objective was to scale the top of a rather large mountain. They started firing at us sometime right after 800 in the morning, and they were still firing at us with live rounds at 1600 hours in the evening. This was very frustrating because all we had were some white dummy rifles and the best we could do with them was to go up and break them over the instructors' heads, which wouldn't have done very much good in that particular time. But it was very good for us to be on the receiving end and to understand live firing and discipline under fire. This discipline and training is very necessary to conduct yourself properly in combat.

During one of our obstacle demolitions, which included demolition of obstacles on land, we had rigged the field with explosives and set the fuses (which were slow burning fuses) loaded with black powder (we call it smokeless powder). Once the fuse lighters are pulled, (of course, the fuse pullers are picked up by boat), there is no way to stop the fuses from going, which are usually set to burn within 20 minutes. It was at about that time that we noticed, while we were observing or watching for the shock to go, that down drove a military jeep to the beach site where we had rigged the field. We were hollering and waving, we'd put the field glasses on and there were two Air Force personnel, it looked like a Major and Captain, walking through the field, for what reason we don't know.

It appeared that this was the end for those people. However, for some reason or another, they jumped in the jeep, and the most they ever got was some shrapnel and some stones, some rocks on their jeep. I imagine they were quite surprised to see this occurring. Where they ever came from, why they got there, we never knew. But they certainly left in a hurry.

On one of our last runs in training, we at that time were extremely tough, and it was getting to the point where we could handle Old Treetrunk pretty well. However, one day Lt. Price took us up a canyon which was full of large rocks. (It was just impossible for anyone to run at any great speed in these types of canyons because the instructor would have to drop from rock to rock, and likewise the trainees following the instructor would have to do the same.) We did have a long hard run into the canyon, and I was able to go into the canyon right behind Tree Trunk. Naturally, all the trainees were trying to get to the front and were kind of crowding to get to the position up front. By this time, it was a rather challenging situation by all. I remember Jim Kenny was—I had let a few enlisted men by, not thinking, particularly some of them that had been a little slower and were having difficulties impressing the instructor force with their physical ability—I let them by, and Jim Kenny, who was one of the class horses, tried to get by, I remember reaching out and hitting him in the Adam's apple with my elbow. Later that evening Jim came up and said, "I certainly hope that you didn't intend to do that up there," and I, of course, pleaded innocent, and said, "No, I was just jumping from a rock. I'm sorry." But underneath it all, the damned son of a bitch hadn't ought to have been trying to get up there.

Anyway, while on the run that day, at the upper end of the canyon, we were informed that the instructors had shot some goats in another canyon. (There had been some wild goats on San Clemente Island at that time. They were domestic breeds but had been running wild on the island.) The instructors had selected and shot a few of the goats for a barbeque, and our task was to go in and haul the goats out of the canyon. I had taught a meats class back in college and had butchered a few animals in my life, and I determined to pass this on to the class. And they agreed that it would only be necessary to quarter the goats and take the hindquarters out.

After agreeing to this we skinned and took the hind quarters back with us in some burlap bags which we had been able to procure from out of one of the instructor's jeeps, unknowing on their part. The instructors had proceeded on to camp, and we were expected to arrive several hours later, and they were prepared to watch us haul those damned dead goats in. The instructors were very surprised when we showed up without any goats and sacks full of quartered meat. So as my part of the punishment, I was delegated to prepare a goat barbeque and believe me, having been out there three weeks without any fresh meat or foods of any nature, only those out of a can, this barbequed goat meat was very tasty and hit the spot.

One of the final phases of training was our four-mile swim. Actually, for the East Coast training (which is held out of Little

Creek, Virginia, and the final phases of that training are held down in Puerto Rico), they swim 7 miles. But then again, they don't have the colder water, which is characteristic of the Pacific. For our swim, however, they took us to sea directly from the camp about four miles. Once there, with the swell and the choppiness of the ocean, there was no way to see directly to the island, other than we could see some of the outlines of the island. It was strictly kind of like swimming by instinct to the camp area.

On that day I was with Doug Allred. He had gained tremendously and had really come on through training. He had come around a long way, and ended up the number three pair, and he could have probably been in Number One, had he had a faster partner than me. The four-mile swim was not considered anything of any big magnitude, except that morning we had done calisthenics and had two problems to do that day, both diving problems, and after the swim we were to go on a 19-mile hike in the evening. So, combining them all together it made quite a day out of it, but then, as I say, the conditioning we had received was superb.

One of the areas of instruction at San Clemente Island that we always seemed to have somewhere between having fun at and being a nuisance, was Black Mike Parker, who was the senior instructor, and taught hand to hand combat classes. He was about 5'7", weighed about 220 pounds, and could be described more or less as blubberous. He wasn't a very effective leader, and he'd always seem to select Jim Kenny, who'd apparently had a little of this type of training, and it always ended up when he was going to throw Jim, Jim ended up throwing him, and he'd always get up and say "Very good, Mr. Kenny. Very good." I do remember though, we'd have to stand in the wind with nothing on but swim trunks, blowing off the ocean, and our endurance was down quite a bit, and we'd be making falls on hard ground, and our bodies by this time were just plumb full of cactus. The island was just covered with cactus, and we had had it in every portion of our bodies, short of our eyes, that I could remember.

CHAPTER XI

UDT Service and First Days as UDT Officer

Finally, graduation day. After a long sixteen weeks, of the 73 men that started there were 15 enlisted and five officers left to go to the Teams. Upon arrival at the Teams, it was a brand-new experience and a new ball game for me. My first impression of the individuals started out: Mac "the Pipe" Boynton as Commanding Officer; his Lieutenant Commander, "Whiskey Jack" Sudduth was the XO. There was also Dave Carse, Eric "The Hun" Melnor, and several other officers. Then we got out and looked at the enlisted men.

There was Tex Modesett who was a WWII hero, had been in Utah Beach in Normandy and had made the headlines, which I'd later seen throwing about 14 or 15 cops out of a bar in New York City. And this was in the headlines of one of the New York papers. And there was Fred Jurik. He was in the 17th Airborne in WWII and was in UDT's in Korea. There were Skinny Carroll and Prince Gallagher. Prince was quite a colorful individual and black man. Chris Morrison, also a black man. Big fella. He'd catch you in a bar somewhere and he'd come up and say, "Well, just because it's dark in here and you can't see me is no reason you don't have to talk to me." He was always very good about the race problem.

I can remember another fella named Danny Cunningham. Danny was a real character. He was a little, short, fat fella. Actually, he wasn't fat, he was just short and solid. But it didn't seem like he could crawl across the ground. All of these fellas, none of whom

I could figure out how they could be the specimens they were, or how they could have gone through training or how they could have upheld the UDT tradition and been old warhorses themselves. But I find out like the old pros, once you do this for so many years, it becomes second nature to you, and you can continue on and do it under some of the handicaps the men seemed to be carrying. Although later I found out they weren't carrying any, they were still awful tough, agile individuals, good swimmers, good land people, good all the way around, superb individuals.

But one day, they were teasing Danny Cunningham in the calisthenics circle, calling him Santa Clause. The leader of the calisthenics circle was Paul McNalley. I'd heard a lot about him for his physical prowess, but he didn't appear to be any huge or outstanding physical specimen. But I later came to find out that man could do more calisthenics longer, harder, and in a quicker time, he could run further or faster, he could swim further or faster than any man that I had ever met in my lifetime. And taking his times that he made then, compared to some of the younger, newer people, now that are outstanding, each of these people are probably more outstanding in one particular evolution, but Paul could do all of it and did all of it. And was a tremendous competitor and great leader.

Another man I remember first day at the Teams was a Petty Officer named Cobb. He had been in the original Scouts and Raiders in WWII. This man was a real instigator and was a platoon Petty Officer and could really inspire and get his platoon put together and create a lot of platoon spirit and platoon integrity. They were the platoon to have to try to beat or excel against if you were attempting to do anything in a competitive nature among platoons.

One of the first introductory programs that was given to a new officer, as he reported to the UDT team (or to the UDT team I reported to) was an invitation by the Chief Master At Arms and several of the Chief Petty Officers in the team to go over to the Chief's Club along with the XO, and Whiskey Jack and a few others, and get to know the fellows a little bit. And Man! What this turned out to be! You start out—you never do eat—it's for lunch—but you start out with beer. A couple of hours of that, you're wishing you could eat, but nobody seems to be ordering, and they're all sitting around listening to some great stories, and then about in the middle of the afternoon they start beer and whiskey. And then, for the evening meal, we're drinking whiskey and whatever. It was quite an event, and it challenged your constitution to see just how solid an individual you were.

One of the first stories in those Chief Club sessions that I can remember was one about Danny Cunningham. When he was on a leave period up in Washington, on a motorcycle (in those days a lot of the guys in the Teams had motorcycles, it seemed to be kind of a fad at that time) and he was up in Washington and ran out of gas in his motorcycle and pushed it into a farmer's yard.

And Danny, being a good consumer of alcohol, and will consume it at any time that he can find it, and met this farmer to ask him for gas, and the farmer asked him in for a homemade beer. They got to drinking some of this home brew, and one thing led to another, and Danny told him who he was. The farmer indicated he had a well he needed to blow. A domestic water well. He wanted to get another layer down to get into some different water, and naturally, indicated that he knew all about well blasting. Which there were no manuals that I saw or no training—so drinking more beers, the false courage gets up, so they go out and start loading the well up, and I since have learned that you'd probably only use about one stick of dynamite at the most, probably a quarter stick. I understand they must have gotten about 10 sticks down in that hole before they got around to setting the blast off, and I guess when this blast went off, rocks and mud and gravel and water all come out of this hole, completely covering and devastating a truck and knocking all the windows out of the man's house, and Danny jumps on his motorcycle and gets down the road just as fast as he could. I guess he was able to get a little gas in the motorcycle.

CHAPTER XII

UDT Operations

This being in the last of the fifties, about 1959, things were fairly quiet as far as actual combat status. There were no wars going on. What would actually occur, there were two teams on the West Coast, Underwater Demolition Team 11 and Underwater Demolition Team 12. One team would take an overseas tour, or we'd call them a West Pac (Pacific) detachment, or West Pac (Pacific) responsibility.

During that year's time, one team would take the half of its men for six months, and then the other half, which meant that each individual in the UDT team would be deployed every 18 months. It was characteristic that, regardless of the war tempo or the political tempo at any one time—(it appears to me, as far as I could tell or read or go back in history from the knowledge that I have)—that since the start of the Cold War, wherever there has been a problem area or hotspot, they have always some way or another used the UDT's either in actual use or in contingency plans, or as a consideration for them.

Primarily, during that period, they used UDT's in Quemoy and Matsu. There they swam radios to the mainland to monitor their short-range communications. There was also what we called "the flap" into Malaysia for the purpose of interdicting Chinese boats, which were infiltrating into that area at that time. I never did find out if they went through with any of the actual blowing up of the boats, but I do know that they left rather rapidly in the middle of the night, and went to a submarine, from there to a seaplane, to another submarine, and had taken Olympic mines with them. These were all top-secret movements at that time, and these fellows would never talk about it or bring on any word of their results. It's really hard to tell what all they have or haven't done in some cases, in their involvement around the world, unless you were actually yourself involved.

A later detachment from UDT 12 made a boat delivery of landing craft to the Laotian government, taking these boats up the Mei Cong River to Viet Than. This became somewhat of an intelligence mission, plus the fact that they felt that these men could get these boats up there. Naturally, you would survey and sound the water for navigable water, looking for any type of military hardware, the general response of the public to an American there, any military activity, or unusual or anything, as it became a damned long report.

I later had an experience similar to this in North Vietnam, which I will get to later. Primary activity was training, supporting amphibious operations overseas, and landings, being in condition and accustomed to various training areas, various types of water, climate, and conditions that could or would be encountered in the operating theater wherever it may be; in this case, it happened to be in the Western Pacific. Then again, there were many times of charting and working in various countries that may someday later become valuable information. I can recall one time having to go to Jakarta on a quick situation and we had some UDT charts, which proved to be very valuable that we had made and passed.

Our deployment and detachments at that time were primarily headquartered out of Yokosuka, Japan. One of our favorite spots was the Club Astor in Yokosuka. One of the favorite pastimes was a wagering proposition where two men put down an equal amount of money, usually from $5 to $50, with the intent to hit the first individual who walked in the door. The first time that one or the other individual refused to swing at an individual walking in the door or that individual he hit cleaned his clock, then the other man would win the pot.

I can remember one time a Lieutenant named Don Balsarini was in this game with another man, and in walked his—for his turn up—in walked a great, big, huge, Shore Patrol Chief, who is a big redheaded fellow. And Balsarini, out of all gallantry, swung at him, and when the Chief found out who he was, he took a little pity on him. However, he took him outside and told him he wasn't going to run him in or make any kind of a fuss out of it, but he said he would just kind of like to teach him a lesson. So, he took Balsarini around the neck under his arm and rammed his head into a brick wall. After that, Balsarini walked around extremely sore for several days, with some stitches in his head. However, it saved a trip in the paddy wagon and the reports and the embarrassment thereafter.

Later the deployment headquarters was transferred to the Philippines, which is still the UDT headquarters. The SEALs did not have an overseas deployment situation as such. Back in the States most of the emphasis was on training, naturally, the amphibious program. But this, by this time, had become mostly repetitious to those individuals to the new people into the Teams. Very little turnover, however, occurs in the UDT's or did at that time. Mainly diving was on water work and that was the primary activity.

Bill Early and Maxie Stephenson (Vietnam, 1965)
(Source: Personal collection of John Randall Stephenson, Esq. All rights reserved.)

CHAPTER XIII

Rebreathers

We had two clandestine rigs, rebreathers as we called them, that we were using at that time. The rebreathers worked by recycling air through a purification process with a recharge of oxygen. A rebreather was effective during clandestine operations because it did not produce bubbles which would float to the surface. This would allow an individual to make a harbor or ship attack, or a sneak attack as we called it, without being detected, or at least it enhanced the probability of not being detected. We had the Emerson, which was a German rig, a very fine rig, it seemed to work in all respects, but it being foreign made, we could not get parts for it and had much difficulty in trying to maintain the rigs.

Pirelli Rebreather

We had another one we called the "black sleeping bag" that was called a Pirelli. It was an Italian rig and was used by the Italians in WWII when the 10th Light Flotilla with 23 men and a beat-up old submarine sunk hundreds of thousands of tons of allied shipping. This piece of gear was not that sophisticated and had not improved much since then. So, it was really on the way out.

Naturally, we had several experiences with the black sleeping bag. Probably the greatest amount of conditioning and self-discipline that a man would ever have to go through was the swimming and the use of one of these rigs, because if you excited yourself, or swam too hard or went too deep you could experience various problems. Over-swimming the rig, you could create what we would call anoxia or lack of oxygen and you may go into passing yourself out. This is where the diving rig got its name from. It was something similar of putting a paper bag over your head and passing out from it. And, of course, diving too deep, past 30 feet, could create a problem. Although sometimes I've known people and myself to take it for a short period of time beyond 30 feet to 60 feet. However, you could go into what we called oxygen poisoning and go into convulsions. Needless to say, this became a very difficult problem to handle, particularly if you were the partner on the swim. The rebreathers had been the cause of more training deaths and accidents than any other one phase that I know of. (At least during the period of my span of 10 years in the UDT's and SEAL Teams.)

Other problems that occurred were that many times you could make mistakes such as not purging the bag properly which meant you had to remove all exiting air and CO_2 from your lung capacity, nasal passages, breathing passages, and the amount of air in the bag. This was done through a petcock apparatus located just below the mouthpiece. It became quite common to become nauseated and vomit in these rigs while continuing to make your swim. Although this was an indicator to not continue the swim, sometimes, by the time an individual gets to wherever he has to go, whether to his safety boat, or whatever it may be, to terminate the swim, he would still have to keep the faithful facemask on.

The Pirelli was used by the Italians, not in the same manner that we Americans used them. They used them for very short distances and actually conducted very little physical activity, whereas we were trying to swim maybe a mile each way on this rig. It became one of the qualifying requirements before you were given complete qualification of use in the Pirelli.

While on a sneak attack or during a sneak attack period with these rigs, I can remember several times going out, making an attack on a ship or group of ships, coming back to our parent vessel, submarine or whatever it may be, and having a headache, perhaps maybe vomiting, laying down, taking a few aspirin and laying down for a while, getting sleep, then getting back up, filling the bag up with new soda lime or calcium carbonate, then getting into another delivery craft and going back at it.

I recall one night during our indoctrination period when we were required to make a swim across San Diego Bay. My partner and I got across okay. However, there was another man and his partner who did not show up.

Finally, we saw that one of the men had lit his flare down below and we could see it. His partner had passed out. We learned later not to do this, but the one who passed outweighed the individual who was conscious and in good position. But he was unable to bring him to the surface. If you have ever tried to handle an unconscious individual on the surface, on land, it is difficult enough. In water, it is much more difficult. So, he had lit his flare hoping that someone would see, and he was detected by a strange pass of the safety boat, which is usually the PR, as I've discussed, with two safety divers, a corpsman, and a diving officer.

As it turned out, the two safety divers had dwindled to only one diver because of some other operation or need or lack of attempting to get another man. The man who was supposed to be the safety diver (he was designated as such) could not help because he had a cold and could not dive. This left no one available to go down to help the other divers out. Finally, the boat engineer, Bob Henry, grabbed an aqua lung in a very hasty manner, still with just removing his shoes and putting a pair of fins on, and by some instinct of navigation reached the bottom and pulled this man up. It was determined by the instructors, after observing the diving officer's logbooks, that this man was unconscious on the bottom for a period of longer than 7 minutes. The man who was passed out was Roger Mosconi. And I always felt that he showed effects of the lengthy unconscious period for several years thereafter. Although today, he is in fine shape.

Another time, Dick Allen, the black all service boxer, and I were at a depth of about 45 feet of very clear water. It was near Okinawa. If we looked up, in fact, we could even get an outline of the full moon. You could almost see the moon, and we were having tremendous success with our sneak attacks by just sitting on the bottom and going up and hitting a ship every now and then, and then returning. Of course, this would not have been practical, and we had explosives, but then again, it was practical in the way that we were playing the rules, in the attempt of giving every ship work and training in swimmer attack defense.

After a while, Dick went into convulsions. I was unable to bring him up, for being a very strong man, we were about the same weight. My main concern was to keep his face mask on and oxygen into his rig and attempt just to keep him alive. While this was occurring, we had a Chief Corpsman named Doc who was able to come down. The Corpsman would not normally dive in these cases. However, we had another Corpsman, and this night he was available to come down. And quite frankly, Doc saved our lives.

CHAPTER XIV

Submarine Experiences

We received our first training in submarine lock out soon after joining the Teams. This, I felt, was quite an experience. The conventional sub and the guppy sub, as they call them, have been converted to be more high speed, which is diesel engine driven, it is again a phase that has been changed because there are hardly any—or will hardly be any someday—any guppy type or diesel type submarines in the Navy fleet. But at this time (the lock out chamber in these subs are the ones that the UDT's would use on a normal sub) were converted the submarine's personnel carrier, however, again they still had somewhat of the same type of lock out chamber. These would only hold the maximum of three people and optimally, two people. You would get into this very small tube affair going up through the top of the forward torpedo room, climbing a ladder through a small hatch into the chamber, and you would close the hatch and turn a valve allowing water to run into the chamber. About the time that the water would become chest high, you would undog the side door. And then this would be probably the first time that you have got on your breathing apparatus. Several times, however, I have made lock outs without ever having air at all. You would use the old blow and go technique, and that we discussed in training. As soon as the side door would be undogged you would then open an air valve compressing the water inside to equalize with the pressure of the depth of the sub outside. At this time the door could be opened freely, and the swimmers would leave the submarine. There is nothing more beautiful than a submarine underwater to observe the boat going by you. Also, at night, to see the vast amount of luminescence that it creates—it is like driving in a snowstorm, or seeing a snowstorm come by you.

We had several experiences on a submarine that were rather interesting. I recall that my first impression in a lock out chamber was that of feeling like a rat drowning. There was cold water coming slowly up, filling up the only cavity that you happen to be in and know. One night we were working with some sound gear. It is easy to leave a submarine, but it is hard for a submarine to find a man to pick him up. We were working with various devices, including an infrared device, and some underwater sound pingers. In fact, we were having good success with this one. We called it a U-Tel. In fact, a man on the surface could even talk to the submarine under the water. And he could make a characteristic sound with another buzzer, and this would allow a submarine to find it and get a bearing and search the man out. Of course, when the submarine would get to you it was a matter of the man or swimmer pair grabbing onto the periscope, because the submarine cannot go at a speed slower than 3 knots. At night doing this was a rather hairy situation. We later found that this piece of equipment, the U-Tel, because the life of the battery, was not practical in that the shelf life of the battery would not allow it to be deployed to any area. In fact, they could not even be kept for a period longer than 2 weeks.

Missed Submarine Pick-up

One night while using the U-Tels and experimenting with them, and trying to establish some operating procedures with them, we were being locked out as a swimmer pair every mile in an attempt for the submarine to go out and make a predetermined turn and come back trying to pick up the swimmers. My swim partner was Ed Reynolds, who was quite a boxer and had tremendously fast hands. Anytime that Ed would start to smile and laugh at you, you could be well assured that you would probably be picking yourself up off the deck. Anyway, Ed and I were locked out of the submarine. It was a nice night, we were about 20 miles from San Diego and approximately 3 to 5 miles from the Coronado Islands, which would be in Mexico.

We could see all the lights of Tijuana and San Diego. The sea was rather smooth. We knew it was going to be quite a while before the submarine would return so we turned our air off and were planning on relaxing awhile. When I looked down and noticed some phosphorescent marks. I could see them further and by that time I got my face mask back on over my face and noticed that this phosphorescence continued to circle. Later I noticed that it had broken surface, and by then I realized it was a shark fin that I saw. So, I poked Ed and told him, I said "Well, in case something bites you, do not ever say your partner did not warn you, because there is a shark coming."

While watching the shark, I remembered H. O. Cunningham's lecture back in training. He said that, in a case like this, you should get a great big breath of air and get under the water. If you could not do that, he said to try to bump the shark on the nose. Some way or another, sharks must have been sensitive to that part of the body. And then, of course, he said, if that does not work, just hope the shark only takes one bite and hope he does not have a buddy that wants to come in either. Apparently, however, I also remembered during the same lecture, that a shark does not necessarily like to eat the human body. After he makes one pass, and of course, if they're not traveling in a wolfpack, cases of a lone shark, as this appeared to be the case, they would only make one pass most probably, and go on about his business.

Also, the type of shark, the breed of shark and the area of the world or water, temperature of waters, and the living conditions that the shark lives in also, I remember, would have an effect on his ferocity. So, I did not have time to get a big breath of air, it did not seem like I wanted to go underwater without my mouthpiece in my mouth or the valve, which had been screwed down on my air tank, shut. In fact, all I had time to do was reach out and bump the shark as hard as I could with the ball of my open hand on the nose. Lo and behold, it worked. The old boy turned, and I can remember he hit Ed and knocked him into me and left. However, it was still over an hour before the submarine returned. We had a long, long wait. And I, being at least 6 feet away from Ed, could see that his eyeballs were as big as two silver dollars. I am sure mine were as big as two coffee cup saucers.

Finally, the sub returned. In this case, the sub had a sounding device that indicated that the sub was making a sound for us to return an underwater sonar sound so that they could receive our sound in the sub's sonar equipment and attempt to pick us up.

As I have stated earlier, being picked up in a submarine is a rather hard task, and particularly at night. This happened to be one night when we spotted the periscope more than—usually it is 5 to 6 feet away from you before you see it and have to grab ahold of it. This night we saw that thing a long way away. I do not know how far, but I am sure it was at least 30 feet, giving us adequate time to grab onto the scope. From the scope or the top of where the scope extends out from the encasement of the submarine, we had a line tied, which was tied at that end, and secured at the other end very near the lock in-lock out chamber.

So, the process would be to grab onto the line and pull yourself down to the trunk, and enter the trunk, which of course, would be full of water, and close the side door and dog the side door, and go through the reverse process of entering the trunk as we did when we filled it. Then, of course we opened the lower hatch and got back into the forward torpedo room. Regardless of the conditions or the type of operations or swim that we had on the outside, it was always a wonderful experience to return to our normal condition. This included hot coffee, a warm room, and a chance to get out of our swimming equipment. However, on this night, as Ed got out of his swimming equipment, he had shit his trunks!

John Randall Stephenson, Esq.

This essentially was the beginning of many wonderful and rewarding experiences aboard submarines. I always liked to travel on submarines. The crews were competent, the commanding officers were not at all hypertensive, and seemed to have more control of themselves and their command. A lot of this, of course, was built in with the nature of a submarine and its own atmosphere. We travelled many, many weeks using them in the Philippines, off the coast of Vietnam, down into Indonesia, Malaysia, Thailand, and off the coast of Korea.

CHAPTER XV

Arctic Operations

One of the more memorable peacetime operations, or more or less peacetime operations, that used to be kind of discussed around a lot, was the Arctic trip. Basically, it was a trip to Alaska. This meant riding the submarine for 6 weeks and seeing almost no daylight. Most of the men would not have a chance to do much in the way of exercises or calisthenics. A little bit could be done in their bunk and the forward torpedo room, but there is very, very little room in a submarine and particularly when there are extra personnel aboard. This throws an imbalance in the entire living atmosphere.

Of course, if the boys down in the sub were doing operations and maneuvers for a long time, the diesel smoke began to take its toll (most of the boats that we worked with during this period, from 1959 to 1962, were diesel driven). Of course, the boats would not be snorkeled nor allowed to release the various telltale smokes that submarines give. The atmosphere, air that we breathed inside the boat, would get full of diesel, including your brain and your eyes. Then from there the crew would not flush any garbage or sewage out of the submarine, and it would not be long before a very deep stench of this smell would also infiltrate the atmosphere along with the diesel smoke. It was something that made one rather admire the submarine people.

Also, it always seemed to be quite a difference in working with a submarine captain who was always willing to support you, and he had the competence and ability to do such. If he could not, he felt bad about it and would overhaul his operation and his crew until he could support our operations. This was a far, far cry from working with the APD skippers who were just the other way—it seemed like they were the other way. They immediately knew when you came aboard an APD, they seemed to think you were a member of their crew and would try to handle you in that manner. This, of course, rubbed the men the wrong way. If they wanted to be members of a ship's crew, they would have never gone through UDT and gave of themselves in the manner that they had in order to become an elite individual.

The trip to the Arctic, or Alaska, as we would say (it's more or less an extension of the island chains up there approaching the Russian country), involved a long, extensive period in this boat. Somewhere along the line we placed some rubber IBSs on the outside of the boat, either through latching or sometimes they had a small ordinance box that was later removed from the submarine, which was placed on the exterior skin of the boat. Then we would do an operation whereby we would walk out of the submarine, unlatch or unstow the boat, rubber boat, and have an inflatable cartridge which would inflate the boat, it coming to the surface with the line still extended from it to the submarine. This would then be a central line for the passage of the swimmers to the boat.

The water temperature in this part of the world is normally around 39°F. It is not impossible, however, to dress, using a wetsuit and what we called a drysuit over the wetsuit, and making wetsuit type or the wetsuit type rubber material, into mittens and being able to actually operate in this water for a period of 35 to 45 minutes.

Of course, this is with extreme effort in doing such. After surfacing and getting into the boat, the crews, which consisted of however many boats that they had predetermined for this operation, would commence paddling to the beach (or it probably would not be a beach, it would be some type of a fjord or inlet with thick ice around, normally, but there would be some beach areas) to conduct a reconnaissance. The purpose of the reconnaissance was to continue to supply landing information for intelligence purposes and use in possible future combat operations, which would be classified as cold weather operations.

It was on one trip that Clay Freeman took some men out who said that, after one boat was stripped from the submarine, the sea swell was extremely harsh. Normally, the swell at boat depths where the boat travels is not noticeable. In fact, the sea can be often very rough on the surface, and the boat could be down deeper than a 50-foot depth, and everything be very smooth. However, on this occasion, the boat most likely was in a shallower depth of water, and there was a different swell action working against the boat.

Of course, the depth that the top of the submarine, or in other words the depth that would be to the depth of the submarine from the surface of water, was usually around 35 to 50 feet, depending on the depth control of the boat. So, when Clay Freeman and these other men finally got their boats up and inflated, they had expended more time, had to put more men in the boats remaining than they had anticipated, and commenced apparently towards the beach to do this survey. Naturally, most of the swimming or surveying could be done in various ways. There were all types of methods of doing a beach reconnaissance and this one method was called the IBS reconnaissance. During this type of reconnaissance, the men never leave the boat. Also, the beach party lines up a series of two poles where the boat paddles out keeping themselves in line with the poles, and they do this in repetition until they cover the expanse of beach so desired or necessary.

They said that it was so cold that there was about a 35 to 50 knot wind after getting up to the surface. This was done at night, and they would—as they would be paddling, the ice would be freezing on their suits and making the movement within the suit and the arms extremely difficult. They said this is one of the closest times that they had ever remembered where every man almost passed out from over exposure. They did have one or two go and they were able to revive them enough prior to bringing them back into the submarine that the men were able to walk back in themselves. The submarine would never surface during these operations. Consequently, it was also a test period for the submarine in the fact that the skipper had to navigate around icebergs. This was a very difficult portion of the skipper's navigation, and everyone had to be alert on the sounding systems and listening systems. It was imperative that the crew remain able to maintain control of the boat at a very slow speed to properly lock in and lock out swimmers.

CHAPTER XVI

Coronado Naval Amphibious Base

Back to the Silver Strand. Coronado, based on its physical geographic location, was an island and more or less of a fill, sand fill, through ocean action over many periods of years. And it had, of course, the seaward or the barrier, outside barrier, to form the San Diego Bay. There would be an expanse, this Strand would run from the mainland as a very, very narrow strip of land, all the way right up to the end North Island Naval Air Base. This distance would be approximately 10 to 12 miles, so it was always. Of course, the Underwater Demolition Teams and Navy SEAL Teams lived out on the beaches in this sandy area, providing sand dunes to run on, the beach areas, and the surf to work in.

Negotiating the Surf

One area that always has been an obstacle in the Frogman's life is the surf. He learns to work with it, to use it, and to become efficient in it, but there is never a time when it does not have an effect upon the operation or on the swimmer's efficiency and abilities. There used to be among us platoon officers in the Teams a kind of standing wager, wherein each platoon officer would perhaps place $25 in a kitty, usually with the Chief Master at Arms. When the surf would get extremely high, and there were 10, 11, 12 or higher feet breakers, the officers would very unwisely select a boat crew out of their platoon to go out and attempt to negotiate the surf.

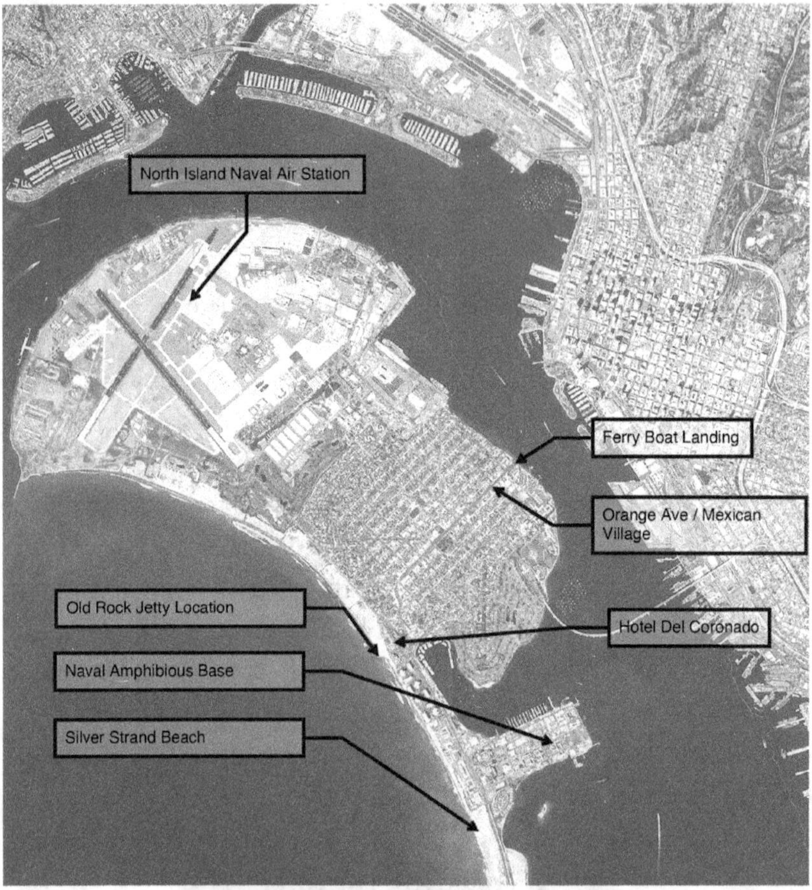

Map of Coronado and the Silver Strand

The first boat crew that would successfully negotiate the surf (it was not necessary to return, but simply to get the boat through these huge breakers, pounding breakers, 2, 3, 4 lines of it), would get the $25 or they would probably make out of it $75—there were usually a minimum of 4 boat crews out attempting to do this. This is essentially very dangerous. A man could be hit in the head with paddles, which could knock him out, and there was the possibility of hanging up in the lines of the boat, although in all these possible danger areas the crews were trained in a manner to not allow this to happen. But there was always this possibility. And of course, if you continued to do these things all the time, finally, somebody's going to get it.

This happened one day when we were attempting to do this, in fact we had determined that it was rough enough not to take the boats, but a platoon would try to get swimmers through the water in the same manner—through the surf line. And so, one day we were out attempting to do it and we did have, in fact, Paul McNalley, who by then was in my platoon, make it through the surf. I remember attempting it, and myself very nearly drowned. I could not negotiate the breakers and I considered myself with my fins a reasonably strong swimmer.

Another boat crew had an individual, a man who had been in the UDTs many, many years, and had negotiated surf many, many years, and physically would have been the last man that you would have considered not to have been able to conduct himself in a manner conducive to this surf passage. However, one breaker got him and it, like anything else, you fool around with it long enough and it can get you. And he came up and we could tell he was in trouble. Paul McNalley was able to get to him after another surf breaker or two had washed him back down, and we brought him ashore, he was still conscious and got up walked over and sat down on the beach. He then fell over dead. This is the time when we still wanted to use resuscitation. We were very industriously working to try to bring this man around, when the team doctor showed upon the situation. (Team doctors I will get into later. I have a long story on these guys.) But this happened to be one of them, by this time we called him

"Quit Smoking, Two Aspirins, Bayer." He came over and pronounced the man dead without ever attempting to look into any possibilities of resuscitation. It just did not seem like this was the man that we wanted to save our lives if we were in trouble. And when a team doctor loses his image and his integrity in the men's minds, he's in a lot of trouble. And it does indirectly create a helluva morale problem.

Women, Dave Carse, and Psychiatrists

Here are stories about some of the women that we had in those days. Dave Carse was a big man, he was a football player at Ohio State and an extremely good-looking man, about 6' 1-2", about 195 pounds, kind of pointed nose, dishwater hair, short and curly, sunken eyes, very defined features in his face, blue eyes and a not as deep a voice, but characterized the voice of Aldo Ray.

I had heard much about Dave and his activities on the beach, and for me it was rather hard to believe. This man was, or rather seemed to be, quiet. Went about his work in the Teams in a very serious manner, conducted himself, he being an officer, at that time a Lieutenant Junior Grade, in a very appropriate manner. It just did not seem that this was the man that would do all these particular events. However, one evening we were at a party given by a group of schoolteachers. A UDT man always seems to have his women. He never really let on, but he seemed to be the kind of a guy that was a little queer. Sometimes he was called that by a psychiatrist.

Of course, we often had a tendency to overreact to studies that a psychiatrist would make on us. I remember one psychiatrist who had conducted studies on us over the years and we got to know him pretty well. I think maybe we gave him more of the straighter dope than anybody else when he asked for it. He later put several articles in papers, one in *Time Magazine*, where he described us as being second on a list of various professions and anxiety levels. But I think this was not necessarily the case. The fraternalism among the men, the hours that they worked together, the mutual respect they had to have for each other, particularly getting into why they must have such a respect for each other, and the Teams being one of the few military organizations that actually allowed the closeness in the officer and enlisted relationships, was not indicative of high anxiety levels. This is again going back to UDT training where the officer was put directly in a position with the class and not marked with his bars and so on and so forth, so that by observation of the instructor force, he would actually be the natural leader of the group. If he could not be, he had no business being in this organization, because he could not conduct himself in a leadership capacity under these more tenable situations.

Basically, most of the junior officers also have to be operators on swims and the more senior the individuals are, officer and enlisted, the more integrity they were perceived to have because of their experience, age, and maturity that you would expect in an operation. Therefore, this would result in a more successful field of endeavor in our tasks. In other words, a buddy pair made up of an officer and enlisted man could not go out with the enlisted man thinking, "Aw God, I've got old Mr. Jones with me tonight, and I've got to look after him all night, or else he's going to drown," or you're going to get in trouble. Likewise, the officer may think, "Well, I can't feel that he's swimming with Seaman Jones, and he's so damn dumb that I've got to do all his thinking tonight." Those two men have got to get in the water and work as a swimmer pair or, as later in the SEAL and fire team components and other types of crews, jump crews, parachuting units, in a manner where there was mutual respect for all individuals and their abilities. It is a matter of looking at a man's good instead of his bad.

So, this was what more or less was the intent with the stripping of all outside environment prior to say Hell Week, putting the trainees through Hell Week and changing the man, a man was never the same after going through Hell Week, in his actual mental makeup. So, through this, I think the misconception of the homo tendencies may have derived. But normally it seemed like they always had all the women they wanted, that they seemed to be in a manner where they could take them or leave them.

CHAPTER XVII

Eating Glass

Back to Dave Carse. This escapade happened one night about Christmas time with the schoolteachers. Dave was there, and I could tell one of the girls, perhaps he tried to put the make on her, and she didn't like it, and he maybe proceeded in a more uncouth manner to see what he could do about it. She apparently gave in or to get something that had irritated her. Dave sat down and plucked a Christmas tree ornament off the tree and commenced eating it. (This was my first introduction to glass eating, which later Dave taught me how to eat glass and I would eat a bit, chew up the glass and swallow the very fine particles of it. I did this for many years thereafter, and even had the team doctor's concurrence that I was more or less eating nothing but sand by the time we would chew up the glass. I never ever remember cutting myself. Of course, again, in the Chief's Club or other areas, this was a good conversation piece, and it was an extension of you thinking you could do the impossible and learn how to do it. We would always seem to somehow or another make a few dollars on glass eating wagers.)

But, when she saw Dave eat this Christmas tree bulb, she could not take it anymore. She got extremely irate and started calling him the big cock clown and just read him up one side and down the other. I remember big Dave said, "Lady, I don't have to take that from you, you damn slut!" Of course, these were all college graduates, a little more sophisticated, type women.

Dave had then turned the entire group against him. The rest of us did not quite know what to do. Old Dave then ran to the door and slammed the damned thing.

Pretty soon we noticed this door had a mail slot in it, with a little flap on the inside for the mail to close after the mail was placed through it. Then we saw the head of a peter sticking through this mail slot, and he started to urinate through it. This, of course, pretty much broke up the party. We were trying to soften the girls' attitude somewhat and were not being too successful. Then, of course, Dave had got the girls to do exactly what he wanted them to do to, they ran to the door and opened it. By this time, he had placed his car on their lawn in front of their apartment. (Actually, they had rented a house.) By then he was busily dragging his car tearing up their lawn.

A Commander's Grandmother

Another time Dave had met a girl down at the Mexican Village one night. He was smooth, and when needed he could conduct himself in a manner that was gentlemanly, and, as with all their women, the guys always had a tremendous sense of fair play. I never heard them talk about their conquests, they did not need to do this, it was not part of their makeup to satisfy their ego. I have never known them to not just take advantage of a woman one way or another. Of course, sure there were isolated cases, couple of rapes and things like this, but this was more of a perverted individual who was psychologically disoriented and would have exhibited himself through any group of society. They were always, I felt, very couth with their women in the general sense. So, David made a little deal with this girl he had met in the Mexican Village, that was kind of what it was all about, and he was drunk.

Of course, she probably did not know this. And like the rest of us, he had probably been drinking, since we always got off on Friday afternoons, and this was a Friday, and he had probably been drinking since noon, and this was probably near midnight. He was just flat drunk. This probably was not noticeable in the environment that he was in. But she had told him what her house number was and the street which was in Coronado. Of course, Dave went to the right house number, but he was on the wrong street. He was on the street one block over from where he was supposed to be.

The house was kind of dark, and for some reason or another, apparently, the door was unlocked. So, he goes on in and kind of finds where the bedroom is and starts undressing. Then this woman starts talking to him, and he starts making some hot, passionate conversation. But it turns out that the woman was in the dark and everything, and he probably would not have known this, but she was the Commander's grandmother. Of course, he kept up the conversation and she appeased him and indicated that she wanted to go get ready. I am not too sure maybe the old gal might not have taken him on, but I don't think she really knew who was in her room. She was actually quite cool and smooth about it, and while she was getting ready, she called the police, and came back in the room. As soon as the police arrived at the scene, Dave had a quick sobering up action and was able to smash his way through the window and ran away. However, they later got Dave because he had left his shoes. He grabbed his pants and that was about it.

The Mexican Village had not yet closed, it was usually 2:00 a.m. when they closed, and we were still in there. Dave then came back, and he was about a sober a man as you would ever want to see. We could not believe it when he came in and said, "Hey, you guys ever try to screw a Commander's grandmother?" We thought it was all a bunch of poppycock, but it turned out later, as we found out as the scene comes to a head, that it actually was the Commander's grandmother. The lady was in her 70s.

The Hun

Another time we were with Eric "The Hun" Melnor. He was a Lieutenant Junior Grade, a Naval Academy graduate, and somewhat of a rebel. His big play was to stand in the officers' club on North Island—we called him "Fuck Melnor"—he would always stand in the officers' club somewhere or in some inconspicuous place in a house, attempting to find a lamp shade. He would stand there for periods of time and in an inconspicuous manner, and people would see this, but would not really pay much attention to it. Normally, his timing would be when it would—the crowd would be rather well done on cocktails or engrossed in some type of presentation on conversation—he then would stand there and just yell "Fuck" as loud as he could. So that is kind how he got his name Eric "The Hun" or "Fuck Melnor."

One time he had been evicted from one of the apartments that he was renting, and it was just prior to a deployment, and most of the young officers were skinflints, they were very, very tight with their money. It just seemed to be something that ran in among them, and it was rather strange because they were being paid higher than any other junior officer in the Navy. (Actually, we received double hazardous duty pay which was a larger sum than a younger pilot would make, or a submarine man would make for sub pay.) But, in this period of time, if he had to move into a new apartment this meant deposits and advanced rents and so on and so forth, so for a period of about 45 days Eric actually lived in the boat pits, which would be similar to a grease pit in a garage or service station, placing some boards over and living more or less as a caveman.

CHAPTER XVIII

Tijuana Bullfight and Jail

But one day Eric "The Hun" Melnor and I and a group of other people went to a bullfight in Tijuana, Mexico. Eric had "Big Tits" Sonya with him. She was a big Swede, and I think every guy in the outfit had probably screwed her once or twice. But she was, or always seemed to have, a shell about her, like she had never realized that she had ever done these things. She really kind of appeared to be very stuck up. As a sophisticated individual, any action that we would take along our animalistic ways, she would look down her nose at, but it had just the opposite effect. She really liked it, she loved it. Like most of the women that I know that have been around the men, they find that basically they like them, they think they are warm, they think that they represent a man to them, and, quite frankly, what I have known of them is that they are compassionate and generally warm people, and as I have said before, with a sense of fair play.

A Matador at the Tijuana Bull Fights (1961)
(Source: Personal collection of John Randall Stephenson, Esq.
All rights reserved.)

But Old "Big Tits" had gotten into one of her snooty moods during the bull fight. We would always go with bota bags, wine bota bags, and swim trunks, barefoot and no other clothing apparel unless a few of the guys would get themselves a serape. She was really giving us hell down there. We were in the heckler section. Actually, a bullfight usually began at 4 o'clock in the afternoon. Somewhere along about 10 or 11 in the morning the drinking would start. We would then be in pretty fine shape by bullfight time. We would always sit in the sunny side of the bull ring, or what would be called the heckler section. We then got to discussing throwing somebody in the bullring, and this was a day that the fights were not too good. Pretty soon the guys got to going on it, and it was not long, and I don't know, I think I was one of the people who was the instigator and one of them who finally got thrown into the bullring. Both Eric and I ended up in the bullring. Since we were in the bullring, naturally, it was—and of course, I had been in rodeo in college, and been around animals all my life, I was trying to play the bullfighter routine. I was not probably doing it in a very professional manner, and the bull was not seemingly getting to me, so, I would walk around and soon they, those Mexican police, do not fool around with you, they came right in and laid the big billy club on our heads.

Removing the Fallen Bull—Tijuana Bull Fights (1961)
(Source: Personal collection of John Randall Stephenson, Esq.
All rights reserved.)

The next place we woke up was in the Tijuana jail. And, believe me, when you get into the Tijuana jail, it is characteristic, they tell you that they throw the key away and you do not get out. So, Eric and I ended up in there. We had been there three or four days and had been studying the situation. We noticed there would be about a period of two hours they would take you out into this sun area, you could lay around and we would try to do exercises. We would be extremely dirty, with beards, and there would be an encased wall, probably 8 feet high, with glass up on top of the darn thing molded into the cement. We noticed that there was no particular concern what we did, and the security was rather low.

So, one day we decided to make a break for it. I could jump that high and grab it, I figured that, so the idea was for Eric to take a run and jump, I would be bent over, and he would jump up on me and make the swing over. By that time a cut, unless we bled to death, was not going to be something we were too interested in. We decided we were going to get out of the damned place. And, sure enough, Eric hit and went over, then I jumped and went over. Man! They really did, they came after us and I can remember they were shooting at us. I can remember as we went around the corner seeing the bricks chipping where the bullets were hitting where we had just left. A very close call.

We eventually made it back to the US. Tijuana was a border town, and we worked our way down to the beach and then actually swam up the coast. At that time the security was not too great along the ocean.

Wishing Well at the Mexican Village Bar

Another time in the Mexican Village Bar I had met a girl named Caroline, whom I had known for several years. She used to date one of the fellows that had since gotten out of the Teams, and she had kind of kept up with him. So, we were at the piano bar and right behind us was a wishing well which people had been stuffed into periodically, and it had been an object of several attractions through the years. I was really engrossed in a good conversation. We were talking about some of the people that she knew, and I was telling her about some of the other fellows that she was asking about. Then a pilot walked up, as I later found out he was a pilot, and asked her to dance. And she said, "Yeah, she would in a minute," but she was talking to an old friend, referring to me.

So, we continued to engross ourselves in a conversation. Then this fellow returned and asked her again. She said no.

And then he turned to me and said, "What has a guy like you got that you can captivate such a beautiful girl as she?"

I said, "Well buddy, I guess it is just like she said, we are kind of old friends."

He said, "Well, you're a shitbird".

About that time, I popped him right on the jaw and punched him out, and he fell up against this wishing well. I noticed that his head hit a little hard and he was knocked out. He had some little wiry damned friend of his, he kept running up, so I gave him some of the same. Both of them just laid there.

By this time, I feel, of course, this was 8 years later or maybe up to 10, since I had had my first escapades in the Mexican Village. The owner and the management had more or less gotten to like me, and I kind of halfway feel that the damned bartenders instigated these pilots into coming up and doing this, because they were, I noticed, seemingly reacting to the point of observing amusement, and they did not really do too much about it. They had a kind of a maître d' and a body shover, a man kind of there to make sure that everybody had coat and tie and shoes on in the place. He came over and pulled the guys outside and revived them a little bit. I did not see them the rest of the evening or anytime thereafter, until about 3 or 4 days later when there was a knock on my BOQ room door during the early evening. The sheriff had issued an assault and battery charge warrant against me.

Navy SEALS Training in San Diego Bay (1963)
(Source: Personal collection of John Randall Stephenson, Esq.
All rights reserved.)

CHAPTER XIX

Assault and Battery Charges

Finally, the deputy went to my room while I sat down and read the warrant to ascertain the damages. I noticed that I had broken one of the pilot's jaws and had knocked a tooth out of the other one. I was not quite sure what they were going to claim or ask in court. However, I was to appear the following Thursday, which was approximately a week later. It so happened that the following week I was to leave for overseas and there would have been no way possible to be present for this hearing. It would not have been in my best interest to ask my CO for a delay in departure from the United States, so I signed the papers and thought about it that night.

Early the next morning I went down to City Hall. By this time, I had made several friends within the department, two or three policemen, through my various meetings in City Hall with several men who had gotten into trouble at one time or another. I was therefore able to arrange my hearing that day in the afternoon. It also happened that I had known the judge through taking or representing or going up with several of our men. I appeared before the judge at the hearing and had taken Caroline down with me in case I thought I needed a witness.

I was in my best uniform, standing before the judge. He started reading this legal gobbledygook.

I asked him, "Judge, is that the part where say I do not need or I do not request a lawyer?" He read it again.

And I said, "Judge, is this where I say I want or do not want counsel?"

Finally, he appeared to be rather irritated, and said, "Yes. Do you or don't you want counsel?"

I said "No, I'm representing myself".

He then read the charges, the same piece of shit that the sheriff's deputy had handed me, and he turned to me and asked me if I had a defense.

I said, "Well, your honor, I don't mean to tear up Coronado, I've lived here for a long period of time, and it's a place I love. I really want to be a tremendous citizen".

Already, I could hear snickers coming from the other participants in the court who had later hearings or arrests or whatever it may have been. So, he asked me the question what unit I was with. I told him who I was attached to.

He said, "What is your particular job now?"

I told him I was the Executive Officer of UDT 12.

He said, "You mean you're not wanting to tear up our town or disturb the peace or any of these things?"

"No, your honor, I'm not."

"Well," he said, "when you hit these men…."

I said, "Your honor".

I by then had realized that if I could average the discussion and the incidents as it happened, then I would perhaps have a chance.

So, I said, "Your honor, I love this place, and I have done nothing in my knowledge to be anything but an industrious, striving citizen within it".

Then he said, "Oh, yes, weren't you the one that brought in Shenners, the man who was convicted of rape?"

And I said, "Yes, your honor, he wasn't convicted, however".

"Oh, that's right, he wasn't. Then I remember you came in on an assault and battery charge with another man, a man named Storz".

Then I said, "But your honor, we weren't convicted then either."

And he said, "Also, weren't you the people that blew the swimming pool apart at the Del Coronado Hotel, and we had a suit on it?"

I said, "Yes, your honor, but we didn't get convicted there either".

He said, "Well, you're a damned slippery individual".

I said, "On what grounds do you base this?"

So, we had various questioning all the time, but by this time the people in the room were laughing. I can remember Caroline having tears in her eyes by now.

And so, he said, "Did you hit these men in the Mexican Village at a certain time?"

And I said, "In the Mexican Village, that evening I was there I happened to notice that the management had purchased two or three drinks for me, and I don't feel that they would say that I was an individual who was rowdy or indifferent to the best interest of law and order".

And he said, "What have you done as a citizen of this town if you say you are the man you're trying to tell me you are?"

I said, "Well, your honor, we sponsor a little league team; we've rescued seven downed pilots out of the drink, underwater, who live here; we pay too damned high of rents to the damned landlords in this place; and we'd be the first ones to protect your ass if they ever came in to play shoot 'em up in your little room here."

The judge just slammed his gavel down on the table and said, "Fifty dollars."

Boy, was I glad to get out of that one.

Coronado Ferry Boats

There was a ferry that traveled between Coronado and San Diego at that time. It was the only means of transportation across San Diego Bay unless you wanted to take a 24-mile drive through Chula Vista and Imperial Beach up through Coronado on the Strand. The ferry was about a 20-minute trip through the wait and going across, which was probably not more than 1-1/2 to 2 miles across if that.

Sunday afternoons seemed to be a time when many of the Frogs seemed to get in trouble. On one Sunday afternoon a group of them were driving around San Diego. I think Dave Carse was in the group, together with a guy named Fillmore, Don Balsarini and Frank Green. They decided to purchase an old automobile off one of the used car lots, take it on the ferry, and then drive it off the ferry. It was possible to do so because they only had a chain across the end of the ferry. (Later they added a hydraulic lift with a pipe since the incident.) But these guys purchased the car and drove on the ferry. They seemed like tourists looking around, but then actually drove the car off the end of the damned thing. It was approximately 36 to 40 feet down, and they stayed in the car and, of course, they were in their Sunday afternoon civilian attire. They stayed in this automobile for quite a period—they trapped some air inside of it and they feel they probably stayed about 5 minutes. Then they commenced breaking windows and exiting the automobile.

It is quite a problem to do this, by the way, because when you break a window in the automobile, the water gushes in and, of course, you cannot swim against it. So, you have to wait until the water fills up the entire cavity and, just before it does, you have to take a big breath of air, which by that time was highly contaminated with CO_2, and try to swim through without a face mask. The water is not clear in the San Diego Bay, but the five guys actually swam to the surface and were able to head to shore. Again the bay, when the tides are running, there is a good current, and just through the normal ascent you would ascend a good distance from the ferry, and most likely from where the ferry dock or ferry landing was located. It would be pretty close to shore. And these guys actually came out of the water and went to shore.

By this time the ferry operator had notified the police, fire department, and rescue agencies, and had ceased to run the ferry. This backed up traffic on both sides of San Diego Bay for several blocks. Then, rather than having the presence of mind to leave the area, the five guys went back to look and watch all the people standing around wondering what was happening. It was not until Frank Green volunteered to swim the end of a wrecker hook and hook it onto the car that someone got wise and considered these five men to be the people who were the ones who drove the car off. Some of the ferry working people had recognized them and then when they pulled it up and saw the broken windows, and saw nobody there, and traced the car back to who had purchased it, even though the purchase was under a fictitious name, they hauled the guys off to jail. It became quite common to go down to bail Dave Carse out of the pokey. It always cost me $25, and Dave was always the innocent man. You could go down and ask him, "What happened this time, Dave." "Well, you know, Max, these people don't understand us. We weren't doing nothing—just standing around minding our own business, and they put the arm on us again."

CHAPTER XX

El Cortez Hotel Swimming Pool

On another Sunday afternoon, the same crew decided to go swimming in the El Cortez Hotel pool, in the nude. And lo and behold, as they were swimming in this hotel swimming pool, (this was in San Diego, one of the more established, older, well-known, with a reputation above average type hotels, and they decided to swim in this thing in the nude), something occurred that they did not plan on. It was some airline stewardesses that were staying there that decided to swim with them. They were having a party also, and they jumped in the pool and shucked their clothes. This thing was really getting into something called an orgy when the management noticed it and called the police department. As the policemen showed up, the guys happened to see them coming in and were able at least to grab their pants, jump over the fence and get into their car. The car was a convertible, so they just jumped over the doors and hightailed it to the ferry.

Social Observations

Just a few notes about our black Teammates. I have great respect for them. They went through training the same as everyone else, did just as well if not better than the rest of us, and they have proven to be superior operators in the Teams. I have served with them in very dangerous situations, and I am sure we would not have been successful without them.

Sometimes, maybe they would have a party or maybe they would be with us at our functions and associate accordingly. We did not have very many of them in our outfit, but then again, looking at the number of Caucasian people in the Navy and in the United States who would be, say, made available, or would have the selection, or whoever would be one of those very, very minute percentages that would end up being a Frogman. Then, at that time, take the same percent ratio of Caucasian to Negroid in the United States, I would say they were well represented. Of course, I've only associated with apparently the Frogman or the black man. I would not say that you could categorize the men to any one segment of whether there were some top ones, and there were some average ones, and there was some low average within our group, just as there were the same kind of us.

I guess what I am trying to get at is that I have tremendous respect for our black Frogmen and SEALs, and I support the current attempts to improve their position in society, but I have always felt that when you categorize a person and tell him what he has or has not had, what he should be or what he should not be, and start making exceptions for it, going back to the old proverb, if you want the government to take good care of you, look what they did to the Indians. And the reason I bring this out, it's only been in the last few years that I have noticed even some of my good black friends seem to have become rather uptight, say in the last year or so. It does not make sense to me.

Recreational Dives

Other Sunday afternoon events. Quite often on a Sunday afternoon we would take what we called a "rec dive," which is a recreation dive, and the Amphibious Base had a boat which could be requested. It was a small patrol boat, having a cabin, with a little larger, about 50 feet long, wooden hull. We considered it somewhat of a luxury affair. It was painted Navy gray, but it had been fixed up pretty well. The Commanding Officer, Mac the Pipe, Pappy Boynton, being a very cool individual in his early 40s, seemed to want to go out with us on Sunday or he was usually going on a rec dive on Sunday afternoon. Of course, Whiskey Jack, who was the XO, would go, and a few of the privileged peons were allowed to go also, particularly, say, Danny Cunningham, who was the boat cocksun and Gary Treolo, who was the engineer. Otherwise, it was primarily an officer setup.

Our favorite diving spot for a rec dive was out at the Coronado Islands. They are located about 17 to 20 miles from San Diego and are part of Mexico. Whiskey Jack always had the ability to dig up some of the best looking women in the world. We all were not too sure what he done with them. In fact, you could follow up on him and probably find a very warm and responsive woman after Whiskey Jack had dated them. We were not too sure Whiskey Jack knew what to do about taking care of them, because on this Sunday afternoon on a rec dive, we went out to the islands and Whiskey Jack went down diving with another partner.

I noticed that Pappy the Pipe he was not diving that afternoon. Instead, he and Whiskey Jack's date went on a swim at the beach. I had since gone diving with my partner and had run onto Whiskey Jack on the bottom. We were working in closer to the shore, and it was rather common for us after we dove awhile to swim to the beach, take off our tanks and gear, lay on a rock and catch a few sun rays. After we surfaced, we just pointed to the beach and the four of us decided to go over and do this, and as we hit the beach and went to one of our favorite rocks to lay on, on the other side we noticed Pappy Boynton bending on Jack's date. I think that disturbed Jack more than I have known any one thing to do to this man. It had a lasting effect on his relationship in the Teams with his Commanding Officer and performance also.

It so turned out that this woman who was involved at this time was a girl named Wendy Wagner. She later did bit parts in the movies and did quite a few commercials. She was a beautiful woman. I can remember in training, she used to come up when we would run along the municipal beach in the Coronado area between the rocks and the North Island fence. She used to come up and run with Treetrunk quite a bit. Of course, we did not really particularly like it, because after a while she would kind of drop out and leave Old Treetrunk's ego inflated a little bit and then he would really move out. It kinda put the hurts on the rest of us behind him.

Sake Parties

Not all Sunday afternoons were involved with women. One afternoon Clay Freeman, who was a very good looking individual, from Dartmouth, very clean-cut young American looking type, extremely polite and courteous, average build, soft spoken type individual, had constructed a garage near the beach in Imperial Beach. (Imperial Beach is located along the lower part of the Strand and on the border near Mexico.) Clay built and decorated this garage into just a normal detached two-car garage, but also into a little Japanese home, with tatami mats and the straw floors and everything was just strictly an authentic Japanese home as one could make it.

At Clay Freeman's garage we had what we called the stag sake parties. There were, I remember, the officers. There was "Buffalo Bill" Early and "Hoppy the Toad," "the Lion" and "the Dog." We all seemed to catch a name at one time or another. One such man was Mel Pearson. We called him "Dirty Mel" or "Test Pattern Pearson." It was quite common to come home in the evening at one of the bachelors' sake pads and find the TV on with Mel sound asleep in front of the TV.

We would ask him various questions like, "Mel, is it a good movie?" "Yes."

"What happened?"

"Oh, it's getting exciting".

And all that would be on the TV at that time, they would have the test pattern on. He got "Dirty Mel" as his name because he could fart something horrible. He used to stink up submarines, boats, cockpits, wetsuits and breathing apparatuses. It was something else, so we just named him "Dirty Mel." Mel could drink fairly well, but he would start getting tired after a while. So, through the evening, I kept drinking this sake, just sitting around the damned table with your legs crossed. I remember Hoppy was taking movie pictures occasionally as the evening progressed, and I can remember late in the evening, eating my sake glass. Finally, toward the highlight of the evening, Hoppy the Toad crashed and burned right during his filming episode with the two floodlights on each side of the camera. He just fell flat on the table, breaking all the glass and the movie camera lights. It's lucky he did not get electrocuted. But we always had a saying that "God protects drunks and fools," so we figured we had a double insurance program going. I can also remember the camera was still cranking away after he was laying there. Nobody moved him, we just kept on drinking that damned sake.

Eventually it did get dark, and we decided to go home, or I don't know, disperse, or leave or something. I was having trouble in my vehicle. I kept passing the same fireplug and, apparently, I was going around the block. So, finally, I apparently stopped, parked my car, and got into a cab to take me home. It turned out that Dirty Mel pulled up to a stop sign and went to sleep with the engine running and the lights on. Eventually the city police came and woke him up. He had apparently been there, it was kind of an off street, for quite a while. They considered him to be inebriated, but at that time they gave him a quick test, made him walk a line and do various reaction drills and he seemed to be able to pass them all. They did not quite know how to write him up, but they were very determined to do such, so they finally gave him a ticket for parking more than 18 inches away from the curb.

Charlie Brown

There was another character we had named Charlie Brown. This was his actual name and not a nickname. He was not a Frog, he was a regular line officer, but a very small, alert individual, kind of a round head, partially bald, and just funnier than hell. Charley was always Dave Carse's big protector and vice versa. It seemed as though Charley was always managing to instigate some adversity whereby Carse would have to end up getting in a fight and quite often getting his clock cleaned. It wasn't that Dave couldn't protect himself and handle himself very well, which he could, but usually if it was a one-on-one situation. However, Charlie would usually get 2 to 3 people lined up to try to whip Dave at once. But one time Charlie kind of ended up in his own flypaper.

We were over at San Diego State watching a man who had gotten out of the Navy and was a good athlete. He was a quarterback for the opposing team, Santa Barbara Junior College. We had gone down to see this individual play and, of course, we did not realize that he had sprained an ankle and had it taped and couldn't play. He was not put in the game and we were hollering, "Bring on Carlin! Bring on Carlin!" The man's name was Tommy Carlin. But nothing ever happened and pretty soon Charlie goes down and begins talking to the coach right on the field during the game. We saw him pointing his finger at the man and shaking it. The coach was ignoring him, and finally Charlie could ascertain that this was the case. So, he came back up and, by this time, as he jumped back into the stands, a policeman came up and started talking to Charlie. The policeman turned it around and he was shaking his finger at Charlie. Charlie all this time had a bag of popcorn he was eating. As the cop was talking to him, he was taking handfuls and eating it.

Finally, the cop made a motion and an indication saying, "Do you understand son?"

Charlie then reached out with his bag of popcorn, offered it to the policeman and said, "Popcorn, flatfoot?"

John Randall Stephenson, Esq.

The cop just picked Charlie up by the nape of the neck and seat of the pants and hauled Charlie out of the stadium.

During that same game (we happened to go in uniform for some reason or another) we had some occasion to wear uniforms but, were probably too lazy to change. Seated in front of us was a Navy Commander, Marine Major and Marine Lieutenant Colonel. They were hollering for San Diego State while we were naturally cheering on Santa Barbara Junior College.

CHAPTER XXI

Coronado Stories

One of Lieutenant Commander Boynton's pastimes was to find a girl, after a few meetings, whom he could talk into bringing into our compound where the duty officers slept at night. He would bring the girl in probably around 2 or 3 a.m. in the morning, and she would then go into the duty officer's room and start making hot, passionate love towards him. The duty officer, as any young, red-blooded American boy would do, rather warmed up to the occasion, and of course, Mac the Pipe would walk in and turn the light on and find his junior officer rather embarrassed. Then again, one of the favorite things to do after this occurred was not to ever bring it up again and the officer would go on wondering about the occasion and what he thought, how much trouble he would be in, and for quite some time. This worked for quite a while, until several of the officers started to swapping stories, and they finally determined that this occurred rather often.

Cable Laying Operations

One of the operations that was quite prevalent during this time (that was in the late 1950's and early 1960's) was a cable laying job. This operation consisted of going to the various stations called the "Pacific Missile Range," which essentially was part of the link up system to the tracking stations to track satellites and space capsules, and other space programs. It was necessary to lay this cable throughout the Range and across the ocean, where we would lay it in several of the Southern Pacific Islands. This was because these areas were to become a central location for relaying and communication centers. Some of the areas that we accomplished these jobs in were in Kwajelein, Wake, Guam, and Johnson Island.

The UDT's function was to make a channel approximately a foot to eighteen inches wide, if it was possible, from the waterline out to about 60, sometimes 90 feet, or wherever there would be the possibility of surf action. They would then lay satchel charges, setting off several series of explosions, in an attempt to create this channel for the cable. After that was accomplished then there became the process laying cement bags in the bottom of the channel and then the cable with a protector over it. This was something in the order of a half sewer tile type thing and then they would lay cement on top of it.

One of the practical applications that came with this process was the ability for one detachment to supersede another detachment and how quick it took them to do the work and how long and how much they could get done with a smaller number of men. This challenge got down to the point where the detachments just quit using any breathing apparatus unless a man was stationed on a permanent job on the bottom. Otherwise, for the demolition laying and putting the ties down, it usually meant swimming with a free dive, or as we called it, the skin dive, with your satchel charge or cable protector or whatever equipment you wanted to place on the bottom, without the use of air or aqua lungs or tanks. This was done to create some efficiency by not having to don the equipment, recharge it, and put up with this kind of operation. Then, this process evolved to where they would palletize all their explosives, cable covers or cement and drop pallets over and then, with the use of air on the bottom, place what was needed accordingly.

We always had sharks in these areas where we were laying these cables. We learned a little bit about them. Usually, they would never bother us for some reason or another. Of course, we were in closer to the beach, and usually the older sharks, the ones who could not stay with the pack, would more or less scavenge around in the inland shallower waters. In fact, we would even kind of name the sharks, because they always seemed to hang around every day, and did not bother us, or never that I can recall bother us. But we always noted that when we broke the surface of the water, it was about that time they would perhaps be laying on the bottom, always swimming looking for something to eat, and noticing a swimmer breaking the surface with the fin or like, working, would take a pass in the direction of the swimmer. However, as they reached the proximity of the swimmer, apparently, they recognized what this was and would turn away. Therefore, I have always felt that H. O. Cunningham and his marine life lecture may have had some validity, because it seemed to be on the surface where we did arouse the shark's curiosity to the greatest extent.

Space Capsule Recovery

Capsule recovery operations were probably the least interesting, exciting, or challenging, other than the publicity that went along with them. It seemed very exciting and intriguing to place the flotation collar around the capsule after splashdown, knowing where it had been and like every other earth being to admire and awe the tremendous feat that had been accomplished. But as far as the actual flotation attachment part of it, the operation was not all that interesting. (It is important to note that there has been a UDT detachment or personnel involved in every manned space recovery that the United States has undertaken.)

Unclassified Moonshot Photo
(Source: Personal Collection of John Randall Stephenson, Esq.
All Rights Reserved.)

The operation involving the Wally Shirra pickup I would say perhaps was one of the more memorable that I can recall. Basically, it was the first time that the West Coast had made a recovery, and we had a chief electronic technician in the Team, one of the brain children who did not have enough sense to come out of the wind or not to piss upwind. His name was Savoy, but he had gotten the nickname Survey. Survey was the most unconscientious individual in the world. We used to watch him and we would have this PR that we always used which had an open personnel deck just forward of the engine which was probably 15 to 20 feet to the ramp at the front of the boat where the swimmers would enter the water.

And Survey would always get dressed at the rear of the boat. It was interesting to watch him get dressed. He would usually be talking most of the time, unaware of his motions in the dressing process. Then, if there was a little swell or roughness at sea, it seems like he would put his tanks and fins on, in total preparedness to enter the water, then proceed to walk towards the front of the boat. In so doing, he would bump his air tanks on the side of the boat, smash a finger if it happened to be there, by someone else in the boat, perhaps fall down, and then trip over someone. When he did this, he probably would hurt someone, knock the control levers, placing the boat in gear, either forward or backwards, perhaps placing someone who had already entered the water in danger from the boat movement. After reaching the ramp of the boat, he was supposed to have had a diving supervisor's check, which would ensure that he was in the proper attire to enter the water.

Quite occasionally the diving supervisor would find that he may have forgotten his regulator, which is the breathing apparatus that allows a man to breath the air from the tanks, and he would not say anything in an attempt to perhaps teach the man a lesson from the aspect of experience. And it would be quite common for Survey to jump into the water and, within a few seconds, surface coughing and sputtering.

Something we would always kind of like to do is when we hit the water, we would be ready and not screw around on top, just throw the mouthpiece in your mouth, and take on off for the bottom. This indicated that you were prepared to go to the bottom. And, of course, there were those of us who always kind of liked to race to the bottom. This required a good set of eardrums, and ear passages allowing equalization.

Anyhow, I don't know how it happened, but Survey ended up on the Shirra pickup as a member of the main recovery team. They have backup teams, there are alternate areas for splashdown in case weather problems occur or they have alternate selected return times in case something is decided against through mechanical fault or some unusual occurrence they have several areas where they would splash these capsules down. Accordingly, there would be perhaps two to three backup teams placed in other parts of the world, in the event that there was such an emergency.

Old Survey was on the main pickup team. Luckily, the aircraft carrier, I believe it was the Princeton, was not close enough in the area, because even though they did not have the entire process as highly sophisticated as they did in recent years, had TV been there, it would have been a historic sight, perhaps, or maybe even a pathetic one, because when the splashdown came, the helicopter got Survey and his crew, there were four people, I believe, who went into the water, and Survey slipped and fell out of the helicopter, and fell headfirst into the water while still trying to get himself re-organized. (There is quite a bit of current that goes along with ocean currents, although the capsule will float along with you, and as long as you drop up-current to it, you can swim to it quite easily. However, if you happen to get past the capsule and try to swim against the current to it, it becomes a difficult problem, although it can be done, and has been done.) But Survey finally got to the capsule and then, when after attaching the collar, it was next necessary to pull the inflation lever to allow the cartridge to inflate the collar. And Survey pulled the handle prior to attaching the collar, and believe me, that capsule practically sank before they got it put together, and the only thing that ever held that capsule to the collar was that two of the other swimmers had presence of mind to remove their web belts and attach the web belts to the collar and to the capsule. This was all that held the capsule afloat. Had they not done this: (1) the capsule would have probably sunk or turned over; and (2) they would have been in a heap of trouble. I guess when they got

Survey back aboard there was more people cussing and bitching and moaning, but by this time they pretty well got used to Survey.

I remember one time later Survey also was driving an LCSSTR, which is a 50-foot boat we used in our later days in the mid and late 1960's for an operating boat. This thing had two 1,000 horsepower turbine engines in it, but we had some electrical problems with the boat. It seemed to always occur through the vibrations of the boat and the water action, surf, swell action on the craft and the actual cushioning of the engine that a breakage in the electrical system would occur. The only person who seemed to know how to keep this thing running was Survey.

One day Survey was out running the damned boat on a test run and, while running it by himself at a tremendous speed, he ran smack dab into a mooring buoy in San Diego Bay. It was a clear day, the Bay was quiet and clear, and he just ran into it. The collision punctured a hole in the boat and threw Survey through the forward window. From that day on Survey could be recognized by the flat nose he now had because of the accident.

CHAPTER XXII

"Doc"

We had a Hospital Corpsman who we thought was about one of the finest Hospital Corpsmen that any military organization, or any organization, could have. His nickname was Doc. This guy we felt was just fabulous. He saved many lives, had helped save mine one night, and did likewise for Bob Henry, who was also a good operator. We noticed that he was always the one that could infiltrate a ship when we had to check the security of ships and various military bases, trying to get aboard and sabotage them or perhaps try to abduct some intelligence materials, writing materials, that would be available to be lifted and returned later after the termination of the exercise.

Doc was always good when you had to go to sick bay. He would be able to prescribe or analyze your problem, take it to the doctor when necessary, and you always felt that you were being taken care of properly when you could get Doc to look at you. He also was very knowledgeable in diving physiology and diving medicine for a layman, a professional layman. He had, on various occasions, gone into the recompression chambers with several commercial divers who were brought to the chambers in emergency cases. Doc functioned as their attendant while going through the mandatory recompression times. This in instances would last up to 96 hours.

Doc's Arrest and Trial

One Friday evening we were about all shitfaced at a place called the Island, which was more or less the enlisted men's hangout. It was also the UDT hangout, located on Orange Avenue in Coronado. I was sitting with Doc at the bar that evening. We were drinking a few beers. Then up walks a lady, and I noticed she looked at him a little bit, went in and sat down at the end of the bar and kept looking at Doc. I poked Doc and said "Doc, you've got an admirer down there," and he did not seem to pay much attention either way to her, and she left. Well, within a few minutes, she came back, and she had a city policeman with her and she made a citizen's arrest on Doc. She stated that he had committed assault and battery and robbed her. She claimed that he had taken several pieces of jewelry from her, and then had knocked her out in so doing it. Well, this we just could not believe, of all the people in our whole outfit, the last person that would have done this would have been Doc. We would not have thought much about it except that the policeman hauled Doc off to the hoosegow. We were then busy running around getting bail for him. Actually, he lived in Los Angeles, his wife and several children resided there, and his father-in-law was the bishop of the Mormon church. In reviewing some of his records, I had known that Doc had gone to seminary school at one time at Baylor, and he did seem to be strong on the religion bit.

So, after the arrest, they had Doc's arraignment and finally proceeded with charging him with the charges he had been charged with previously. We went to the trial. This had to be one of the funniest things I can ever remember. This was because, when they started pulling up the UDT members as witnesses, it went something like this:

"What's your name?"

And they would reveal their full name.

"Where were you on the morning of the incident?"

"Well, I was on a helicopter drop and pick up."

"Well, do you remember at that time of Doc being there?"

"Well, no, but he was in the other planeload."

"Do you remember Doc being in another planeload?"

"Well, I don't know, but Skinny was in that plane".

"Who's Skinny?"

"Oh, Skinny Carroll".

So, they would call up this guy named Skinny Carroll and say:

"What's your name?"

And he would state the name.

"Your alias is Skinny, is this correct?"

"Yes".

"You were in the second planeload of helicopter drop and pickup. Was Doc in this planeload?"

"No, but I saw him that morning as I went to the plane and I'm sure he was in the other plane."

This thing just kept hopping around, they were sure that Trader Vic or some other individual had seen him that morning and, of course, each time they said he was with this or that group and each time they would try to ascertain who this man was, who was Trader Vic or who was Prince, and then, of course, try to ascertain what they were doing. Then they would cross examine everybody as far as, "Did you see Prince there?" Or, "Did you see Trader Vic?" Or "Did you see Skinny?" Or "Did you see some other individual?" But during cross examination, luckily, everybody pretty much came out and said they had not actually seen him. Then, all of a sudden, they got Chicken McNair, who came out when it had looked by this time that things were getting a little more involved than we had even thought about.

By the time that we had gotten down to stating the fact that we had always held a muster in the Teams on a platoon level, but several of the more senior enlisted people and administrative people in their capacities, say as our Corpsman, our Senior Corpsman, would not probably have been on the formal or official muster and, of course, this included a summons to the Executive Officer of the Team, Whiskey Jack and a few other people, to determine the actual procedures and proceedings. Through all this time, Doc still did not have anybody who actually testified that he was there during the time of the alleged incident, which was a period of 8-10 in the morning. But we just felt that, by God, he was there with the group.

As it turned out he was there by 9:30 a.m. and had participated in this helicopter drop and it wasn't until 9:30 a.m. that he was first recognized and testified as such. Pretty soon, as it looked like it was getting a little more critical and things were getting much more involved, it turned out that they had this Doc guy registered in several motels in Tijuana over the weekend, perhaps maybe in another motel up in Los Angeles with several different women. It started looking like a Hyde and Jekyll program, and pretty soon, Chicken McNair, who was a good friend of Doc's, got up on the stand and said, "It was me who registered in those motels with these women. I erroneously used Doc's name."

Of course, people who knew Chicken could well believe that this could have been true. So, it looked like maybe we were going to get Doc off the hook in some areas where some of the skeletons were coming out of the closet. Then the prosecution asked Chicken to write Doc's name on a piece of paper to have a handwriting expert see if he could determine whose signature this really was on the motel drafts. Then, right there in court in front of everybody on the witness stand, Chicken started to write Doc's name and had the audacity to ask how to spell it. Quite frankly it turned out that this situation fell apart rapidly.

Doc was convicted. What had happened was he had answered a call in a want ad section about some jewelry sales from a woman. He went by the evening before and looked at the jewelry with the woman. He then came by at 7:30 a.m. the next morning and committed a crime where he actually did rob the woman. He took the jewelry items and hocked them in a jewelry store on his way to work and was at work by 9:30 in the morning. Doc really did not like breaking the law. In Chico, they say he was very disturbed while he was there. From that day on I have always remembered this incident and have a mutual distrust for anyone other than those people whom I totally know their entire living habits.

CHAPTER XXIII

Demonstration of Operations

Demonstrations of operations were always a big thing, always have been, to attempt to impress the public for recruiting purposes. They were also conducted for various political moves and just for general interest. We would always do it up well with a big show. If there were any senior ranking officers in the group attending the show, we would always make sure we got a spray of water on them. It seemed to inflate their egos to get a little action again after a good shot having been behind a desk for several years. Of course, we would always put on our best, but we could probably do about three-fourths of what we said we could do. This was primarily because we were usually ill-equipped.

Development of Submersible Units

We often lived out of a salvage yard during those years. We were not equipped with any sophisticated kind of equipment, and we were really searching for missions and tasks and other things to do. But it usually was not hard to find things to do and keep those kinds of submersible people busy. In fact, we had one submersible unit which was a powered by batteries. With this submersible, a man would just actually lay on top of it and ride it. He could then use this to dive and go along at about 3 knots. The submersible could also carry 2 people laying on it. You would run the controls in a little cockpit inside with your hand laying on top of the unit. It was essentially built from a jet fuel tank.

Building and using this type of submersible was an indication of what we could do. We called it the Drut, which is "turd" spelled backwards. This was one of the best pieces of equipment that we ever had. It was built by the guys, in particular by a man named Bugs Bolen, who was smarter than the average bear when it came to matters along this type of equipment. In fact, during that period, we had several prototype boats made by Aerojet. These boats were pieces of shit, and we just never could get them to accomplish the specifications that were required of them. But this damned Drut would work all the time. We used it in sneak attacks on ships and harbor penetration, and as a swimmer delivery vessel if necessary. It was acceptable to use it on and off submarines. The Drut was really the first submersible unit that was an effective piece of gear for use in UDT and SEAL Team work.

Texas Demonstration

One of our better demonstrations was when we were down in Dennison, Texas. Of course, Texas being what it is and the people down there were extremely hospitable, gave us everything you could think of, let us come into some of their private clubs, and gave us booze and food. They were just tremendous people. We also felt that we had established a tremendous relationship with them.

On this day we gave our demonstration in a small lake. We had boats down there and were giving a demonstration of a drop and pickup and submerse to the beach. They had allowed us to blast and fell a tree that was on a small island in the demonstration area. As the narrating officer was telling everyone how we were very closely calculating all the explosives, Dave Del Giudice and myself were the two people who were actually loading the tree. We were to take eight whips around the tree with prima cord, which would be the normal way to cut or fell a tree. Instead, we snuck a couple satchel charges with us and we laid these up around the tree.

During the narration when it came time for the shot to go, the narrating officer raised his hand and said, "There it goes." Because of the blast, the whole tree and part of the island had just disintegrated, with huge branches and limbs and branches flying all over the crowd, and on top of the cars. Believe me, had this happened in any other place but Texas, it would have been a catastrophe. But this just flat impressed those Texans down there, and all I can remember them saying is, "Golly, what a show!" We were asked to come back to Dennison every year thereafter, and some years we did manage to get back, others it was just impossible.

Swimming Pool at Hotel Del Coronado

One time we managed to crack the swimming pool at the Hotel Del Coronado giving demonstrations, and with that shot we also knocked few windows out of the hotel proper itself. I think that one ended up costing the government $10,000. While discussing the Del Coronado Hotel, I would like to bring up a situation that happened one night. The duty officer that night got a call from a lady who said she was at the Del Coronado. She said she was a guest there, and that there were a bunch of UDT men swimming down on the rock jetty in the nude, and that she would like to have something done about it.

The officer proceeded to explain to her that he felt that it was not any of our men, however, he would check it out, and check his operations, and if it would happen by chance to be somebody from that outfit down there, he would correct the matter immediately. He then hung up the phone and proceeded to check it all out. He came up with the determination that it was impossible for any UDT people to be down there, as there were no programs scheduled at night and he was reasonably sure there had been no parties or beach parties that would lend to them being on the premises that she discussed. So, it was not long that she called back and asked what he was doing about it. He again assured her that there was no one down there, and he also said he had sent a person down in a jeep to check it out. The person had found no one, military or otherwise, in this type of attire.

And she said, "Sonny, are you calling me a liar?"

He said, "No, Lady."

So, finally through a period of short conversations, she hung up. It was not long until the police department called and asked the same thing, and the man went through the same program. Later, I got the story from a friend of mine who was on the police desk that this lady had actually called the desk. The lady stated that she had called the duty officer, which the duty officer had mentioned, and then she went on to say that he asked her if she had wanted to press charges.

She said, "Yes, she did".

He asked her if she were willing to come down to the station and sign the charge sheets.

She said, "By all means, she would be down there in a little bit".

He then said, "Well, lady, you realize that this report goes from us, and then it has to go through some of our higher authorities, and then it transfers over to the Navy and back down, and it's a rather serious thing that you're stating here."

She said, "Yes, she realized that, and she was fully aware of everything."

He said, "Well, there's another thing that I might like to ask you right now. Do you have a grudge against these people or anything?"

She said, "Oh, no! I have nothing but the greatest admiration for them or did have until this incident."

He said, "Well, could you identify—do you know any of these people?"

She said, "No, I don't know them, but I can identify them."

He asked, "How's that?"

She said, "They have great big watches and real little peters!"

UDT Operations Continued

Several of our West Pac operations included training other UDT's, primarily the Taiwan UDT, the Korean UDT, and the Philippine UDT, which was called Filipino UOT, which meant Underwater Operations Team. We always had a tremendous relationship with most of these people. Quite a few of them went through our US type training, although the foreigners do not have the stamina that the American does. Of course, they are away from their natural environment, and their religions, and various areas like this, and they have not had in many cases the proper pre-training. Then when it gets down to just actual day in and day out go go go go, well, it seemed as though, primarily, most of them—they'd start falling out. Although there were some extremely competent and outstanding foreign people, which I will get to later.

CHAPTER XXIV

Korea: Duffy's Bar and Cousin Weak Eyes

While we were at the Chinhae Navy Base in Korea, the big bar was called Duffy's. In Duffy's there was a prostitute or a bar gal we would call her, named Cousin Weak Eyes. Cousin Weak Eyes had been the topic of discussion from year to year, detachment to detachment, and she could be described as a rather skinny girl. I truly feel she was probably pretty much of a nymphomaniac, and she had bad eyes. She had tremendously thick eyes. One night we were in a big card game at Duffy's, during a party that had been going for perhaps 2 to 3 days on the weekend. People were coming and going and raising hell, but it still was the same card game. Cousin Weak Eyes was also sitting around clipping a little money from the guys as they would make a few winnings and want to fall out of the game. They just would bend on her right off over in the corner in the room.

One night Cousin Weak Eyes was there at Duffy's. She kept saying she "no wanted no fuckee, no fuckee." Naturally, you would have to be pretty drunk to take her on anyway, and it was normal that when the guys were on top of her, she would be laying there chewing gum and reading a comic book. Every now and then she would politely reach up with some clothing apparel in the near vicinity and clear the steam off her glasses. So, this is the way she got to be Cousin Weak Eyes, although she would always look at a guy and kind of squint and ask him if she had ever screwed him before, because I don't know as if she could see 2 feet in front of her, or ever did recognize a guy that she knew. Although she always knew the name, she could remember the name, or touch them or feel them and remember them in that manner.

One night, Ace Bowen, he decided he wanted to take her on at this one particular time when she was saying no. So, finally, Ace kept on.

One of the guys finally said, "Look Ace, leave her alone, she's got the rag on."

So, Ace said, "Aw hell no! That ain't gonna stop me."

Of course, old Cousin Weak Eyes, seeing a little possibility of making a few bucks, decided it did not bother her either. So, the next morning old Ace wakes up and he's got blood strung from one end of his T-shirt to another. We watched him and he runs to the shower and looks in the mirror and starts looking at his face.

He then says, "My God, man, did I finally win a fight?"

We said, "Well, Ace, it depends on how you look at it."

He said, "What did I do last night?"

When we told him, he could not believe it, he thought he had been in a fight and won, because if he had not won, he would have been beaten up. He could not accept at all what he had been in. To this day Ace cannot live that down and wishes he could.

Crazy Amy

In the Philippines, it was Crazy Amy. Crazy Amy was kind of cross-eyed and always had a little dry snot around her nose and was always drunk. She was a rather thin, slim woman, and if she would clean up and square herself away a little bit, was a reasonably attractive individual. When she was sober, she had a tremendous mind, good conversation, tremendous knowledge, witty, in fact, she could play a good game of chess. It was very enjoyable to play a game of chess with her. But when she would hit the bottle, it was curtains.

The first time I remember meeting her, the first thing she said was "Mr. Stephenson, I'd like to fuck you." However, she did not say it in front of the people that she was involved with. It so happened to be that I was with a couple of embassy people from Manila, and this was in Olongapo. We had gone out for dinner. One of the guy's hangouts was called Swanky's, and we had gone over there for a drink. Then up comes Crazy Amy with snot hanging out of her nose, and kind of all messed up, and she come on with this statement. She would always attempt to try to get you in a corner somewhere when she was in this state.

However, one night, I had a drinking bout with one of the Ensigns. We were going to see who could out drink the other, and I finally lost. I still feel somebody gave me a Mickey, because I woke up the next morning laying on a door which was kind of on top between two sawhorses. They apparently were doing some sort of remodeling of the bar. I had had my shirt underneath my head with my billfold in it. It was there, I had not been rolled or robbed or anything like this. As soon as I started coming around, I could tell it was midmorning and knew I had been there for quite some time, I looked around and there was Crazy Amy. She had sat there all night actually protecting me and seeing to it that I was not hurt or molested and was taken care of. Of course, she got me up the next morning and got me some Alka Seltzer and a few things like this and took me in the bar and started getting me going. I'll never forget Crazy Amy, because there are many, many other stories of guys getting in these situations and it not turning out that way. They did not have a loyal Crazy Amy to look after them.

UDT Sports

Athletics was a big thing in the Teams at that time. Usually, it never extended much beyond intermural athletics, base type, although our volleyball teams actually competed and won in national competitions. They had won the Inter-Service Competition, and I think, whenever they went into open competition on national basis, they might win a first round or two of a tournament, but they found they were far inferior to the top volleyball teams in the nation. In fact, the compounds as they were built, and existing UDT facilities are actually built around two volleyball courts. Therefore, this game kind of grew up with the UDT's as they grew up. It is always characteristic to have a volleyball game during the lunch hour, or just play for hours and hours and hours.

Of course, I previously mentioned some of the boxing and boxers that we had, although Dick Allen went by far the furthest in it, we did have some other pretty fair boxers. San Diego was a boxing town, and some of the fellas did pretty well in it. Football was also one of our greater sports. Although this was just tag football, touch football, we had a lot of fun with it. Normally, each team would place a team in competition for the Admiral's Trophy on the Naval Amphibious Base. Naturally, each team would, this being UDT 11 and UDT 12, probably be bracketed into two different leagues.

UDT 12 Football Team (Maxie Stephenson, Top Row, Third from Left) (1961)
(Source: Personal collection of John Randall Stephenson, Esq.
All rights reserved.)

When UDT 11 and 12 had a football game, it was an event of the year. Everyone in the entire area, both in the civilian and Naval communities, turned out for this game. Sometimes there would be up as high as thousands of people just to watch it. Basically, it was not that there was a grudge, it was just a matter of two equal teams just playing football that were able to meet and both on this same caliber quality of individual. Basically, there was not much to it, except for a group mastication. This tag football later led us to a game called rugby. Mainly it was introduced through the Ivy League influence and some of our contacts with the British and Australians.

One of the highlights of this program was a rugby game where we played for the southern California championship against the Los Angeles Rocks, which we later found out was loaded up with Los Angeles Rams football players. I cannot, at this time, remember who all some of the players were, but some of them were the named linemen, linebackers, and backs. From this game we ended up with two broken legs, a broken collarbone, two broken arms, several broken noses, two broken jaws, and for some strange reason we did inflict some injuries on their team. They had a fella, I think Deacon Jones was one of them who was playing, he was a big black man, and we had a like individual called "Bear Tracks" Allen who was about 6'4" and weighed somewhere in the neighborhood of 250 pounds. So, this turned out to be a very competitive game. Of course, they won. However, they knew we had been there.

CHAPTER XXV

Instructor Unit

After several overseas operations and operations within the Teams many of us found it rather challenging to become an instructor, at least I did. I requested duty as an instructor and was then selected and sent over to the training area. I functioned as Whiskey Jack's right hand man or his second in command.

When I got over there, I became what they called a hate symbol. I don't really know why. I guess it was a matter of my enthusiastic instructing procedures, which I would question as to whether it was good instruction or mainly psychology. I remember one of my introductory lectures to the trainees was I told them to look at the man in front of them, look at the man on each side of them, and look at the man behind them, and at the end of the training period, which would be 16 weeks later, they would find that the man was not there. They just looked at all four of the men that they had just looked at and realized they probably would not be there. Then I introduced them to a sock full of sand, which we kept under the podium. This was kept there in case somebody was caught dozing. He could then rest assured that the sock would be thrown at him. We explained that the sock would be later introduced as a weapon that could be used as a means of ingenuity, it being something that was on the body proper it could be filled, this could be used as a weapon sometime at a later date. I also indicated that I had a very poor throwing arm, and I would most likely hit the man next to the man I would be throwing at, so if they found their buddies were sleeping it was in their best interest to keep everyone alert.

"Tadpoles"
(Source: Personal collection of John Randall Stephenson, Esq. All rights reserved.)

I explained to them exactly what a UDT trainee was, and that their actual names were "Tadpoles," and they were called Tadpoles throughout training. I also introduced the word "Hooyah" to them and, as they went through the training process, they would shout this word. It would become a household word with them and have various connotations as to how bad they hurt. We explained that a trainee was so low that one day we were swimming in a very, very deep ocean, and we were diving to about 20 feet and the water was very clear, except it was becoming rather hazy down there. Then we looked way, way down and we saw a great big, huge whale turd floating by. Then looking further, beyond the whale turd at a deeper depth, there was a trainee, who was the best trainee we had ever seen. We stated that was an indication of their position in life for the next 16 weeks. We gave every man a chance who had still been used to Mama's tit to get up and walk out right then and there.

We also indicated to those trainees who felt that they needed assistance at any one time that we always had the old ambulance on the scene, particularly on our runs. We would have the ambulance full of alcohol and ice, and if any of them happened to get in trouble with heat prostration, they would be given a ride in the old wagon with a load of alcohol and ice on them to cool them off, with the trainees running behind them, helping them on. So, if any of them were not in condition, they could rest assured that the good old instructors were going to take care of them. And after the ride in the wagon, we would have an alcoholic doctor who would be more than welcome to take care of them during their stay in the hospital, which was somewhere between 2 and 3 weeks. We then told them that anybody who did not feel that they could run 17 miles at this time had no business being in the training.

Quitting UDT Training

At about this time, we would introduce the trainees to the instructor force. The instructors would all come out and smile and act like goody-good guys. Then we would turn the trainees over to Dr. Barber. Dr. Barber was a Corpsman who had seen duty in WWII and Korea. He always had a great big, huge wad of tobacco in his mouth, hands in his pockets, slouch on the stage and start out by saying, "Youse guys, your first and best way to get your training is to pray to the Sun God, because you will be like cold cunts, which means dead meat, bub, dead meat." He explained to the men that if they got blisters not to worry about it because we would adequately place them in San Diego Bay and in the ocean to give them adequate time to soak and get that good salt water in those good old sores, and not to report to him until their knees started swelling up and they saw a blue line in the affected area, meaning short of blood poisoning. We also explained that if anybody quit, no one else was to talk to them or were they to talk to anybody within the group. Once they had quit, it was over with. They were to get down the road, go back to their nice, warm barracks, nice, warm bunks, nice chow, girlfriend down on the beach, and be pussies for the rest of their lives.

Doc Barber was to be the class proctor. He actually lived with the men. Quite frankly, the whole idea of this introduction was to try to start the psychological process where the man had to have a complete grasp of himself and to start considering the moment and try to consider what we were trying to do and take the program from there. The men had to put all out, in that training program, but we still wanted a certain amount of trying when the situation seemed impossible, because every man sitting in that classroom had no idea whether he would make it or not. He certainly thought he would or could, or else he would not have been there. But it was only that select few who could really take one day at a time and perform for that day, then worry about the next day. This is exactly what it takes for the missions that are assigned this group of people. There are very, very few projects where you can ride a bicycle, put on your tennis shoes, go work out for a little bit, go out for 2 or 3 hours in a ball game, hang up the old jock, take a nice shower, get some good food, and go to bed. It does not work in this outfit. There may be days of cold, there may be days of hardships, there may be hours behind the lines, hours in a prison and hours getting into a prison. This was the type of man we needed. It is sort of like playing music. It does not take a lot of members in a band to make good music. It was the same way with the UDT trainees, and their missions and objectives.

I became one of the instructors who was a runner. I was not like Treetrunk where I could endure long periods of sustained running. I still had a more powerful set of legs, a little faster, so I became what they called a jackrabbit runner. I would love to run fast, run slow, run over sand dunes, run over water, and continue this lack of pacing ourselves throughout a run. Another thing I used to like to do was stop immediately, try to get a trainee to run into me, and put him in the leaning rest position, circle back behind him and then run over the top of him with my boots.

CHAPTER XXVI

Wolf Crook Cigars

Another trick I used to do was with Doc Barber, who used to like Wolf Crook cigars. I would run with a pair of combat boots, which were higher and heavier to run in than the gear that the trainees were running in, and I used to smoke these cigars on the run. During the run, I would always try to position myself in the forward portion of the group in order to let the smoke filter back behind the men. I think that perhaps the smoke did not bother a lot of them, but there was the psychology of having that cigar up there and the continuous chain smoking of the cigars, where Doc Barber would drive up in the jeep and pass a cigar out to me as soon as one would get burnt down to a butt. Several times after that, a number of the trainees made comments about the horrible cigar smoking that occurred during a run.

Also, another thing I used to like to do during log PT and Hell Week as the trainees were laying on their backs, standing the log above their heads, and there would be several crews, I used to like to run and jump on all the logs as they were held by the trainees. This was great fantasy. Another area, I liked to set up diving and a diving contest, setting up several rubber boats, making a ramp to run down, and more or less of a diving boat to leap into the mud. We found this very satisfying for the instructors.

Trainees on San Clemente Island

One time during which the trainees were not performing was at San Clemente Island. We had given the trainees a real tough problem, where we had them paddle the entire length of the island, and they were to accomplish several difficult problems, all out of a rubber boat, living out of sea rations and moving completely hidden without any tents, without any sleeping bags, without any conveniences other than their operating gear and what could be effectively placed in a very small backpack. This was a backpack that could be swam with if necessary.

We had the men working on the first day. They started out with a tremendously rough sea to paddle the length of the island, arrived at their problem late and were late getting done with their problem until the early hours of the morning. Throughout the night we continued to harass them, and every time we could find them, we would get them up and try to capture them. They would escape because we purposely let them get loose, so that they could set up another camp and re-organize. Then they would have to go through an entire day returning to their explosive caches that they had made, trying to return to where they may have placed some of their operating equipment, still composing themselves and organizing into a problem where they could effectively accomplish a given task that they were assigned to throughout their period for those 3 or 4 days.

Training Rebellion

During this time, there was Chief Burton down on that portion of the island and he and another Chief, Lonny Price, were over rigging a chase off situation. We had not given them Chase Off Beach as was characteristic for this part of the training. We were going to work it into this battle problem as we called it when, as every ingenious young individual does, the trainees finally were able to spot a vehicle that the Chief had left. They discovered that he had left the keys in the thing. So they took his—outright rebellion—stole the vehicle, drove it to the other end of the island where our base camp was and came in. I had been out all night and was extremely tired. However, I was probably not as tired as I am sure the trainees were, but this happened to be my seventh class and I probably was not all that enthused about the continuation of being a trainee instructor seven times over.

    I was sound asleep in my plywood hut. I was at that time, the senior man present and in charge of the training camp because my boss had been taken back to San Diego for political reasons. I could not believe it, here they were, the guys had about 4 logs of horse cock (baloney) under their arms, several loaves of bread, and big piles of cheese. They were running around madly and shooting blank ammo. This occurred after they had raided the galley and got into the cellar boxes containing our food. I was awakened by a simulated hand grenade in my bunk, which, when it exploded, blew the end of my sleeping bag all to hell and blew one of my toenails right off my goddamned toe. I was so damned pissed could not believe it.

    As I came out of my hut, bleeding all about my foot, and so angry I could not even hardly see straight, some guy straightened me up by banking me on the back of the head with the butt of a rifle. He put me down and then they took off in the truck they had stolen. They were heading to another place called Wilson Cove, which contained an Air Force facility and a Navy test facility. They were going there to attempt to get several cases of alcoholic beverages. It seemed like they were pretty damned stupid, which was indicative of their leadership at that time, because they did not do this before they decided to raid us. I thought it would have been much more ingenious to have made proper plans, which I later told them about.

    I was chasing them down the road in a jeep and I did not take the time to get any other instructors with me. I could see they were accelerating the truck to what I felt was near dangerous speeds, so I backed off in my jeep so they would not wreck and kill themselves, although at that point I didn't care. Then they went on into this cove.

Well, it turned out that I knew the roads in there apparently better than they did, because I pulled out at the end of the road on the exit on the way out, crossed the jeep across it, and there was no other way they could pass the truck through. They came driving up and I pulled the senior man out and told him to get his ass down at the other end of the island and do it immediately and quit his screwing around. When he got down there to muster up at China Cove, and I planned to give him further instructions.

On the way down to China Cove, I could not quite believe what had happened. I really did not know quite what to do. About this time, I happened to see coming up over a hill in the distance in an area perpendicular to where the road ran, the two Chiefs who had had their vehicle abducted. I waited for them. They were as pissed off as I was and, in fact, they couldn't even talk. So, by the time we got down the island the senior trainee was there, and he was standing out like a big bull chief on his first big rebellious warpath. He felt he was going to still negotiate or explain their grievances, which we were not about to let that kind of bullshit interrupt the process.

I told them to go back to their dressing area, wherever it may be, and the uniform for the next problem would be lifejacket and bootees. (Bootees are small rubber foot fitting dress that you put on to protect what we called fin burns from the fins.) And, of course, they came back out in lifejackets, face masks, web belts, swim trunks, fins, you name it. I explained to them that the uniform was lifejackets and bootees.

The second time they came out with lifejackets, bootees and swim trunks. I again explained that the uniform was without trunks. So, then they came out with jock straps, shorts, you name it. I explained that was not part of the uniform either. So, finally, they all came out in the nude with their little old penises all shriveled up. In fact, I can remember a Mr. Ruth telling me that, "Mr.

Stephenson, you explained that at San Clemente Island we would not harass them any longer, we were out to do practical problems."

I explained to him that he had not necessarily conducted himself in a manner that was consistent with a grown man, and he had in fact turned into a candy ass. That is when I told them that they were like a bunch of Arctic cunts, plain old cold meat, and I intended to keep it that way.

Happy Hour

Well, for some reason or another, it turned out that I came up with the thought of Happy Hour. I explained for all the men to get in the water. This was cold Pacific water, which was over their heads, but located in a cove where I could walk along the beach or on a shelf up above them. From there I could pace in front of them, explain that they could not sing, they could not talk, and they could just tread water. Treading water in a bootee is like trying to basically swim with a mitten on and you cannot use the water in your appendages to its best advantage. So, I paced in front of them while they were in the water, looking at me. I explained what my interpretation of a Happy Hour was. It went something like this:

> "Happy Hour is basically a social function to relieve pressure. And there are pressures that now exist among the instructor force. We have noted that the performance of our trainees is less than desirable. This creates much worry because they will later become our swim partners, our buddies in combat, and the men we have to socialize with from here on out. So, it involves a liquid with a cold object inside this liquid. Since we cannot quite have this in the manner as normally prescribed, today we will provide the same thing. We have provided a liquid, which is this beautiful ocean that you are now in, the solids are your bodies, so we have everything necessary to perform the Happy Hour. Now, as the Happy

Hour proceeds, people get to talking and it allows them to release themselves within, so this is essentially what I am going to do. You guys are a bunch of pussies as we have so said at several times and will continue to say it. You are like a bunch of Alaskan cunts. Now, let's take the incident that you just performed and develop it into a great working group, where is the leadership? The leadership prevailed to rebel. In rebelling, it's fine. What did you accomplish in rebelling? Nothing! It's when you can do something and do it showing that you have hair on your ass, some imagination, some performance, to create a cause and a goal in the best interest of all concerned, then you rebel. Rebelling was perhaps your release; we feel that it was not in your best interest. I am sure that you will find as you go down the road years later that it did not fit into the big picture. What was a problem to you at the time of taking the truck will not be a problem to you years later. As you look at the big picture, you will find that what is significant today are those that can observe what is significant, those that can do something about it, and do it in a clever and proper manner. Those are the ones who will succeed. Certainly, you must have felt this to be clever, you must have felt it to be brazen, but as far as I am concerned, it was easy for you take that truck, it was easy to go up and shoot up the camp, and it was easy to take the food. Then you were like a bunch of dumb bastards, you did not even plan that well. If you really wanted to rebel and do it in a manner that we would have felt more of you as men, you would have hit the booze hall, the chow hall, and Wilson Cove. Then gotten the hell out, done the trick, without stirring any commotion, and then went off and hid in the mountains here. From there you should have created a problem, set up a defensive perimeter and made us come and get you. Then we would have had some respect for you."

Believe me, during this discussion, these men's minds were rolling over a million miles. It was a very effective I felt, in retrospect a very effective approach. Sure, it was some brainwashing. This is what it's all about. It's whose program is doing what. This basically was a method to assert ourselves, to assert the capabilities we felt we had as instructors, to implement our professionalism, and to produce the finest UDT men that the Teams had known in their history. This is what anyone strives for, what is best can be better, and what is better will be best tomorrow.

CHAPTER XXVII

Instructor Politics

When Whiskey Jack and I first entered the training unit, we were not too cognizant of the political pressures, the pressures that are involved in empire building and from the Naval, "Don't rock the boat, don't create any waves" program. If you do not conform to paragraph 1, in accordance with reference A, of serial number 100,000 Zulu, then you do not get our duty points at the end of the month. And we knew what we had to develop in training, we had both been operators, we had both been around, we both were intelligent beings, and had, we felt, an understanding awareness. So, we proceeded, in not the proper manner or in accordance with military doctrine, to re-orient and re-establish in the long term a training program that would produce an operator in the Teams.

Regular Navy Man

Our first encounter of some adversity was a Senior Chief Bosun Mate named Stan Antrim. I had him in training and had absolutely no adverse comment concerning him. I thought he had a tremendous military bearing, tremendous delivery with his instructing procedures and proceeded in the image of a trainee as that man who could carry out any duty anytime, anywhere. Well, this was our first encounter with what we considered the regular Navy man, and my first encounter with the hypocrisy of these type of individuals. At first, we thought he was so perfect and had performed his duties so well that we began wondering how we were going to perform our duties as the leaders of this group of men, which by the way, turned out to be 12, four officers and eight enlisted men. We decided right then and there that we could never fill another man's shoes, we have to be ourselves, and we have to proceed about our business. And we were elected to be the leaders of this group. We decided that if Antram was the military man that he should be, then he would conform and follow in.

Well, it turned out to be just the opposite. He carried a point of animosity, and we found out later he was more or less shitcanned out of the Teams over to the trainee area, because nobody really wanted to operate with him. The image and the performance and the example that he could set, at least, from the front, was very ideal, so they felt that he was properly placed. We felt that this was also the case, until we discussed the point with him that if he would conform, if he would go along with us, we would not have any problems. As it turned out, he more or less looked at us as a couple of wild young officers that he would have to take care of and have us do things his way. This was not the way we understood how leadership should work.

As we delved into the program further and further, we saw that he had been Black Mike Parker's leading chief and could see where he had completely overrun Mike Parker and understood how he could do so. And if he had been a man of some analytical abilities, he would have understood that he could not do this with us. We felt that we gave him adequate chance to do so. As we got into it deeper and deeper, we could see the psychological disorientation within this man's mind. And, true, it was developed through years and years within the Navy process, but we found where he falsified records, and he had out and out lied to individuals. So, we decided to fire him. Whiskey Jack was cold blooded enough not to make an issue of the situation, so he reverted him to taking care of the gear, more or less like on a football team, he had been the equipment manager, a step down from an assistant coach. Chief Antrim had some Naval buddies that he had built a good relationship with, and we found out that we had made a mistake by making him equipment manager. We should have worked him out in another manner. But this did not turn out that way.

Our second mistake occurred in a rather odd manner. We stepped into the last part of one class where they were going to San Clemente Island for their final phase of training. We were still kind of prone to UDT habits on the beach and ended up in Wilson Cove at the Officers' Club, this being an Air Force facility, getting flat-assed drunk. There was Whiskey Jack, me, and Dave Bramble. For some strange reason, we could tell through the evening that the reception was not too warm and apparently Dave could too. As he went to the head, he passed by the officer's laundry facilities, and apparently some Air Force Officer made a comment to the effect that, "What in the hell business did we have there, and who did we think we were drinking with those people?" Dave took offense to this, and pissed in his laundry, standing above the washing machine, and told him in that manner who he thought he was.

This immediately threw on the alarm—all switches turned red. The Major going through his Colonel, and the Colonel going through our superiors and our superiors in the middle of the night, not knowing what to do, back in San Diego. Later on the next morning, we had the executive officer of the outfit, who was a displaced and frustrated pilot, we called him Happy Jack or Smiling Jack because he always smiled, fly out to pick us up with Commander Hashmo. We did not know why, and they did not explain why. They just said we had to go back to San Diego. Ironically, we left Dave Bramble, the man who had urinated in the washing machine, in charge of the trainees. We felt this was rather inconsistent with good thought.

We eventually made the long trip back. Whiskey Jack and I were sitting in the back of this SNB (it's a two-engine aircraft) and the two Commanders were up in front flying the plane, talking to each other. I do not think Jack and I said one word on the way back, wondering where we were going and what had happened and so forth. We landed on the damned air base and they transported us in a black car to the amphibious base. Then we were sure they would put us in a room and tell us to stay there or something else, but they just turned to us and said, "Can you be contacted the rest of the weekend?" My God, here we were being allowed to go on liberty when, essentially, we were supposed to be punished.

Military Inquiry

After returning the San Diego, we learned that this incident on San Clemente Island had created a formal investigation. I mean there were the tape recorders, there was a Command Captain, a Navy Captain, two Commanders, a Marine Major, two Lieutenants and several enlisted men all involved wasting time investigating the entire UDT process. Little did we realize that there were a lot of snakes in the grass out there, waiting to kill us, and it was not with a gun. It was just jealousy, animosity and lack of imagination, which is a typical thing that comes within a bureaucratic system. It was all there, right in front of us. We went through 5 days of investigation, and in the military court, the officer who is the interested party or the individual being investigated, who in this case happened to be Whiskey Jack, can become by his own choice, a member of the board. He has no voting rights, but he can cross examine to align a situation, such as if say, there was an accident on the beach while you are undertaking a run. The questioning would go like this:

"You ran these trainees for a period of time, when did you stop?"

"Well, we stopped more or less when we felt we were ready, as our observation of the group you're running in".

"Is there a time limit when you stop?"

"Not necessarily".

"Do you run at intervals, say like 15 minutes start, 15 minutes stop?"

"No, we run them as far as we possibly can take them".

"And when one man falls out, as this man did, did you realize he was in trouble?"

"No, I didn't realize he was in trouble because he was in front of the group, and we normally concentrate on the rear of the group."

All these answers indicated that they thought there was negligence involved. Negligence is a big thing in the military. If they can prove negligence, they can get rid of you. Competence, baloney. They assume you have it and that is all the further it goes in the assumption. They never used competence too much. So, then they continued to say:

"What was the temperature that day?

"Well, it was 98 degrees".

"What was the humidity?"

"I don't know".

"Well, did it feel damp?"

"Yes, the humidity seemed high."

Perhaps they would even call in somebody else to discuss this to say what the humidity was that day by some weather forecaster or someone of professional nature along meteorology. Then someone like Whiskey Jack would say, "Did you take the men into the surf? What was the temperature of the water? Did they have time to cool off?" He put this thing back into perspective to preserve his integrity, that was what was being investigated.

The inquiry went on for several days. Then, because I was second in command, I became the officer who was investigated. I continued to answer questions, and I was on the stand for 5 straight hours. All over pissing in a damned washing machine. But that was only the heading of a long period of built-up jealousy, as best as we could feel and describe it. When I finally finished the investigation at the last, I asked if I could have a statement to put in the record. The response was, "By all means."

John Randall Stephenson, Esq.

I explained that I was not a pervert, I was not abnormal and, if I was, then I must question my own self. I grew up in a common mid-American town. I participated in common activities, developed by the system. I proceeded through the universities that had been developed by our system, and I went on to perform in those functions as a common average individual, still a product of the system. In other words, I felt I was an American. I went through the training programs as prescribed, so I cannot see anything further than the common American man. I believe in God, I believe in our flag, and I believe in doing an excellent job. And if what we had given them in this investigation does not indicate that we have talent, that we have ability or that we are not product of the system, then perhaps I had no use in the Navy, or in my university, my high school or my city, or as a citizen in this town or this country. Therefore, I must elect to do another thing, because I felt we were making sense.

Another point of hypocrisy throughout this investigation was that we, by this time, were very aware of what was occurring. We felt in our minds it was a railroad job, much as I'm sure Commander Bucher found out and various other Army individuals in a current day event and many other commanding officers that never made the papers. People out trying to do a job. Maybe some of them were wrong, maybe some of them were way wrong, maybe some of them were damned right.

CHAPTER XXVIII

Warfare Books

I can remember reading a book by Otto Skorzeny—we read a lot of books about commando warfare or guerilla warfare. In fact, I think we had perhaps the best library and the greatest knowledge of any junior officer in the United States military, State Departments, or anybody in the mercenary racket, in background natures of this type. But Skorzeny, who was a tremendous commando for Adolph Hitler, he was one of the men who conducted, or planned and was able to spring, Benito Mussolini from a prison after the people had wised up in Italy and placed him in a prison. Skorzeny went into the prison and brought Mussolini out to keep him alive to keep the structure of the military organization going. And he said that he, after transferring from the front lines to the rear, was associated closely with the upper command of the Third Reich, but he could also see the men out in the front lines not being equipped and see the lack of ingenuity and integrity in planning and operations. He could go back and see that, if everybody's paper basket is empty, if everything was processed in a proper manner in the paperwork, then the generals in the back line went home, thinking they had done a good job for the day. It is this same attitude that disturbed me about the concept of an all-volunteer army. We thought we were great, if you did not think you were great you had no business being in this outfit. We also felt to be great you had to have some knowledge. This just did not occur by running around on the

Strand swimming 50 miles, diving 150,000 feet, eating all the whale turds and beer bottles we could get and punching out anybody we saw. It was much deeper than this.

Perhaps some of the results of us doing this were some of the frustrations perhaps that we had observed, particularly from the command level and the senior positions that you would get into. But we studied books on various subjects, from Sitting Bull, the Horse of Troy, Tito, Lawrence of Arabia, and sinking of the Armada, right on through. We always knew when we could work on an element of surprise, when a small force with a cause can always beat a large force. They can hold them. This whole concept is not a matter of paying an amount of dollars to receive an amount of protection. A war or a taking over of a people or a misconception or a disagreement between two societies, two nations, two clans, two tribes, there is a reason for the war or disagreement, and if there is not a reason for the war or disagreement, then the one side that does not have a reason or cause, will lose. This doesn't fit into the scope of a volunteer military force, we're kidding ourselves, and I do not think this country is anywhere near the degradation of the thought of this idea.

As a result of the investigation there became a normal time of delay while all this processing was going on. I also remember getting back to the snakes in the grass and the awareness of the railroad job at present, and we also reacted. We used to pay the drivers of the cars to bring back information about the investigation. We were supposedly sworn to not discuss, not to divulge, not to carry the proceedings within that room any further than the room itself. We found out that they were plotting against us, through the drivers of the cars.

Whiskey Jack went up to the school during this time, and he happened to be sitting in another room. We were looking for friends, and he had found one in a man named Commander Hashmo. Whiskey Jack was sitting in Commander Hashmo's office discussing the matter, getting some counsel from Commander Hashmo who was perhaps giving a little turncoat within his own organization.

He had no reason to like or dislike us. He likewise felt we were being ostracized somewhat. True, we had made some mistakes and we could later see them, but we were fighting for the continuance of a good trainee, the continuance of a good Frogman, and basically to express ourselves as people with a cause. While sitting in this room, Whiskey Jack overhead Old Smiling Jack discuss some very important areas in which it looked like we were getting ahead of the game, and Old Smiling Jack just went "Shit! Those goddamned bastards!"

Now, here again, was another indication of the hypocrisy. We were sworn, sworn to the Bible in that room, not to divulge and through our own intelligence any information that we created or obtained. But just blandly overhearing this statement by Smiling Jack who was in the staff immediately above us, then we knew what the name of the game was. It could be described as shit. Not all was lost in that investigation, in fact, I think it takes sometimes these types of things to shake an individual up, to make him look at himself and see who he is, what he has got to do, and where he thinks he is going. But this also created a disturbance in the training that was going on at the time. Whether we had the support of our instructors, whether we were going to lose the drive and the desire of the trainees, and the entire psychological pattern of training, was in jeopardy.

CHAPTER XXIX

Admiral Charles K. Duncan

One night we were at a command performance cocktail party, dance, or dinner dance situation. I would say this was somewhere around 6 weeks later after the inquiry. Admiral Charles K. Duncan, who was in charge of the training, and the training command overall and had the overall responsibility of our group, was there. Throughout the night, Whiskey Jack and I felt like we were rather ostracized, although we felt we had made some friends, we could start seeing some people, feeling, and realizing that we had a cause, and we were not idiots or animals.

Later, in the late hours of the evening, I went up and discussed the matter with the Admiral, which supposedly took a hell of a lot of guts. Whiskey Jack danced with his wife, and I said, "Admiral, what in the hell happened in the investigation. I'm not concerned as to what happens to us because that will be brought out as to right and wrong, but there are mens' lives involved, there are the professions involved and there are matters at hand that have to be taken care of."

Immediately he started to cross examine me on certain areas to see if I would reveal something or discuss something while being somewhat inebriated. Naturally, we felt we had given the members of the inquiry our straight shot and had nothing to cover or hide.

So, he said, "Well, in due course, son, it'll all come out."

The following Monday morning, I felt that something would arise from this, it just does not happen that you more or less encounter an Admiral at a cocktail party and not have some sort of repercussion, and by all predictions and analyses, it is normally bad. I can remember being out that morning. I had already alerted, and made a friend with Commander Jim Williams, the Admiral's aide, that I thought perhaps sometime through the day the Admiral might request me. I was out giving a deep dive to the Marine recon, and I explained to him that we could waive the deep dive and it was not important to the Navy, but it was important to the training process in SCUBA training that the men, regardless if they were Marines, UDT or whomever they were, received the proper training. So, I requested from the Admiral's aide that if the Admiral called me, to please ask for me at approximately 1400 in the afternoon. Which was when we were scheduled to return.

Sure enough, I arrived at 1400 hours with a message on my desk to report to the Admiral. I had earlier put a set of utility greens on. I was wet because we had hit spray in the ocean on the way back from training and, naturally, I was in my working attire. I went over to change into my uniform, and I came to the conclusion that what a stupid damned thing to do, to change into a uniform to go get my ass chewed. So, I just went up there in my damned utility greens. As I walked down the passageway past these colonels', commanders', and captains' desks, all of them looking down their nose at me in the improper uniform to visit the Admiral's quarters, I walked up to Jim, and he just pointed, smiling, right on in.

After I entered, the Admiral asked me what I had been doing. I explained that I had been out on a dive with the Marine recon. He seemed very interested in it and asked me if I would like a cup of coffee. I took one, I was shaking.

He said, "I see you're wet and perhaps cold."

I was not shaking because I was cold. He asked me to take a seat, then he reached over, pushed a button, and said, "Send the bastard in." The man he sent in was Captain Cait, the Commanding Officer of the base. I feel I could describe him as a very religious man, a good man, but an overgrown boy scout who never really jelled into a leader. A blob, somebody who could have been somebody, but never made it because of the system. And again, if you fail in front of the system, it is not the system, it is you who failed.

Captain Cait then stood in front of the Admiral, clicked his heels (I had never seen a Navy Captain click his heels in my life) and said, "Yes, Admiral."

And the Admiral reached in his desk, it was about Christmas time or very near, and took out a box and said, "Here, go wrap this damned thing, and I want it back at 1500," which was an hour later, less than an hour later. And, actually, Captain Cait went over and wrapped this himself, as I later learned from the women who were working in the wrapping department on the base.

The Admiral turned to me, and he said, "Now you, son, did you see that mealy-mouthed son of a bitch in here?"

I said, "Captain Cait?"

He said "Yes."

"Yeah, I saw Captain Cait."

He said, "Now, son, what do you think when I call them in like him to sit down and discuss battle problems, war problems, problems that necessitate a professional in our business. You know what he's going to tell me? He is going to sit there for about 15 minutes and try to figure out what I want, what I think is right, and he is going to "yes" it. When you have a group of people who are specialists in fields and you bring them into a room and ask them a question, you want a straight answer, not an answer that has come from somebody else, but an answer that has been soundly thought out by their own mental process, and that man won't do it. Now, for our problem, son, I read through that investigation Sunday. I cannot answer your question as to what to do, because as you well know, this thing has got to on a higher level."

Little did I realize that this investigation had gone on to higher authority, where I do not know, but he said, "As far as you're concerned, I want to talk to you man to man, don't you ever change.

You may get in trouble, but don't you ever change, and you're going to be a man, my son."

And you can well believe I walked out of that damned Admiral's quarters looking at them damned son of a bitches sitting at those desks, and there was 2 feet of cloud under me.

Later, Admiral Duncan became a great friend of mine as he accepted me more or less as a second son. He later became Chief of Naval Personnel.

Laugh Silently

Another time, while conducting the great passage, surf passage, down at the rocks as an instructor, this class of trainees had tremendously beautiful weather. There was not hardly a breaker all that afternoon and it could be considered a frustrating point because the trainees seemingly were gaining on the instructors. But the instructors were irate because they felt the trainees were not getting the proper training that was required when they got into the field.

Finally, late in the afternoon, a huge breaker started rolling way out and came in and smashed a few trainees into the rocks. As it was coming, we all laughed. We laughed hard and I guess I laughed harder and more sadistic than anybody else. There were some tourists or guests of the hotel watching this process, and they reported me to some type of hotel authority which later got to Admiral Duncan. Admiral Duncan called me up and asked me to discuss the matter with him. My explanation was this: I proceeded to tell him the frustration of the waves and the surf and the training and the need to do this, and when it came, because of the feeling at the time of the instructors, it seemed to be a natural thing to have this humor because we were humans also, we had the right to laugh. We knew what we were doing, and I feel that if a private individual, not knowing anything about something, can create an incidence like this then there are some terrible, terrible things occurring within our system. The Admiral just said, "Next time, son, laugh silently."

CHAPTER XXX

Training Dives—Officer Vias

On another occasion, while giving an indoctrinating Pirelli rebreather training class, which was to be conducted in San Diego Bay, at a depth of 15 to 20 feet, we were giving the trainees bounce dives. These dives required the trainees to go to the bottom, purge the bag and return to the surface. This was a very elemental, fundamental process.

Well, we had a Filipino officer there named Mr. Vias, who was one of the few good officers from a foreign country that we had had. This man was outstanding. I can remember one night when he had four enlisted men with him in this training program and, during Hell Week, the four enlisted men did not come out for a muster, they were all sitting on their bunks. (As I said before, this is when the men quit.)

I went up and said, "Mr. Vias, your boat crew is forsaking you. You have created a disillusionment in my mind as to what kind of man you are."

He said, "Yes, sir," and very calmly, in a confident manner, went into the bunks. He did not say anything, but only pantomimed a knife chopping a head off and these four men rallied quickly and immediately. He had done several other things that we felt were very clever and very good. Now his process may not be considered as culturally advanced or ethically sound as some other programs, however, he was able to take care of the situation when required.

Mr. Vias had caught a cold and we realized that he'd had a cold because he had taken Neo-Synephrine to clear his nasal passages before the dive. During the dive, he could not get to the bottom, he could not clear, and he, being a very proud man, continued to attempt to get to the bottom. He eventually made it to the bottom. However, for some reason or another, he took his face mask off, and was still trying to clear his ears on the ascent. Instead of exhaling the air through his passages, he was holding it in, therefore allowing the air within his lungs to expand which essentially created a minor embolism. When he reached the surface, he passed out. We pulled him aboard our boat and had very quickly diagnosed what we felt was the problem. Although we were not doctors, we could not tell. But he had the symptoms we were taught to know that indicated this may be the cause. Within 7 minutes, not from the time that we retrieved the man, but from the time he left the boat into the water, we had him in the recompression chamber. Then the physician, old "No Smoking, Two Aspirins, Bayer," showed up on the scene. By this time, we had Mr. Vias down to the equivalent of 150 feet. Doc Barber was in the chamber with him. The man then became conscious, started breathing, and seemed to be okay. He was talking, said he felt pretty good, and naturally we knew he would go through some pneumonia symptoms. Then "Two Aspirins, Bayer," said bring him up, he is okay. Doc Barber in the chamber continued to shake his head no, no, and he brought him up on the quick diving tables.

The Bends

Now if there was any damage to the lung tissue, the passage of nitrogen which creates the bends (decompression sickness), could not occur as rapidly as it would if there was normal lung tissue. This situation would have prescribed to use the alternate diving tables. We discussed this with Dr. Bayer, and he continued to insist on bringing the man up, like he was afraid or he was scared. At about the equivalent of 100 feet the man passed out again. Again, Dr. Bayer did not respond appropriately to what we felt was the real situation. I asked Whiskey Jack if I could take command from the doctor, and he said if something ever—if this man continues and dies or something happens, you will be hanged. Let the man die. Doc Barber was inside the chamber screaming, I was screaming on the outside and this ass continued to allow this man to come on. They put him in an ambulance to take him over to the hospital at Balboa, which had no diving facilities whatsoever. We at that time, other than a submarine tender, had the only diving medical facility in the entire southern California area. The man died on the way to the hospital. The autopsy indicated that he died of the bends.

Now, anybody knowing anything about diving physiology knows that you have to go beyond 100 feet and stay at that depth for quite some time or, if you are at 60 to 90 feet, you have to stay down longer than there is any air type system the UDTs had at that time to create the bends. There was no way possible this man could have had the bends in 15 feet of water. They had a small investigation, medical investigation, and washed the incident out completely. This is when I first started taking assessment of the medical profession. We had good doctors, sure, fine doctors. But this revealed to me that again, regardless of whether you are a doctor, lawyer, painter, plumber, secretary or banker, there are good and bad, competent and incompetent. And this has always led me to question why an incompetent medical man can receive the same gratuity that is afforded that profession.

We had another doctor named Dr. Bower. He missed a week on the Strand when he was supposed to be there and was with us at San Clemente Island. Certainly, the task involved, the calls, and the use of his knowledge would not have been anything too great. It was certainly not considered a challenge to be there, but rather than making the best of it, he felt was degraded. One he day got pissed off and started just flat beating and punching the walls. He knocked 3 holes through my plywood hut.

CONCLUSION

These stories end abruptly because no further transcripts from Maxie Stephenson have ever surfaced. Maxie continued his career as a Commander in SEAL Team One until January 3, 1967. We then moved to Nevada and began our lives there.

As mentioned earlier in this book, from 1967 until his death in 1982, Maxie served in the United States Naval Reserve. He began service as a Commander and headed up a Navy Construction Battalion, commonly referred to as a "Seabee" Battalion. After successfully leading his Seabee unit for several years, he was promoted to the rank of Captain. He also participated in several Arctic operations in Alaska and Naval war games in Alameda, California.

Maxie was recommended for promotion to the rank of Commodore in 1982, which, at the time, was a rank in the Admiralty. He was always regarded during this time as an intelligent, bold, and effective leader whom the other officers and enlisted personnel trusted and liked.

Despite his successful career in the Navy, Maxie seemed to struggle in civilian life. He held many positions in the private sector, including working as a ranch and livestock appraiser for a large bank and owning and operating an explosives manufacturing business in Reno, Nevada. As indicated in his early stories, because he was raised on his family ranch in Wyoming, he was passionate about raising livestock, particularly cattle. However, despite his love for raising cattle, several crashes which occurred in the livestock market in the 1960's and 1970's resulted in significant financial losses for Maxie. He never completely recovered from those losses.

Maxie Stephenson died in an unfortunate diving accident off the coast of Maui on October 12, 1982. By then he had remarried and adopted his new wife's daughter, Michelle. Everyone was shocked to hear of his passing. He had the reputation of being invincible and larger than life. For years afterward, I would hear rumors that he was still alive and seen at times in Southeast Asia. I also heard theories that he had committed suicide or was killed because he had become somewhat of a loose cannon in the Naval Special Warfare community. I do not believe any of these stories are true, but rather are the answers that people invent to hide their sadness and disbelief in losing an officer and teammate of such extraordinary abilities and popularity.

At the time of my father's death, when I was 23, all I knew was that I had lost a father whom I was just beginning to know as a man. We attended services for him at Saint John's Presbyterian Church in Reno and later attended a service conducted for him at sea near the U.S. Naval Amphibious Base in Coronado. Both my sister and I struggled for years with the loss, but, being Maxie's children, we never gave up. I went on to graduate with a bachelor's degree from the University of California, Berkeley, in 1985, and a Juris Doctorate degree from Golden Gate University in San Francisco in 1990. Upon graduation from law school, I served a judicial clerkship for the Seventh Judicial District Court in Nevada and then served as staff attorney for the Nevada Legislature for over 30 years. My sister Janell eventually graduated from the University of Nevada, Reno, and later became licensed as a marriage and family therapist in Elko, Nevada.

In the end, I hope all readers of this book have acquired a new and insightful appreciation of the thoughts, experiences and challenges faced by Maxie Stephenson and all the other officers and teammates mentioned in this book. Together, each of them made a significant contribution to upholding the high standards of the Underwater Demolition Teams and the early development of Navy SEAL Team One, created January 1, 1962. By doing this, Maxie and the other officers and teammates helped weave the long, complex, and often colorful fabric that represents the modern-day Navy SEAL Teams. I thank each of them for their dedication and service.

SERVICE RECORD

The following information sets forth the official Department of Defense service record of Maxie Stephenson. It includes the period from 1957, when Maxie was drafted into the Navy, to 1967, after he had completed his service with UDT 12 and SEAL Team One. It is important to note that, after separating from service with SEAL Team One in 1967, Maxie moved to Nevada with his family where he continued his service as an officer in the Naval Reserve. He remained in the Reserves until his accidental death in 1982. During this period, Maxie was promoted to the rank of Captain and was recommended for promotion to the rank of Commodore. He did not live long enough to accept the promotion to Commodore.

Service Record of Capt. John M. Stephenson, Jr., USNR (DD 214)

1. May 3, 1957—Enlisted for term of 6 years.
   Service number: 332-77-22

2. September 4, 1957—Accepted commission as an Ensign, USNR, after completion of OCS in Newport, Rhode Island.

3. August 1, 1959—Completion of UDT training in Coronado, California, with major courses in:
   (a) Demolition of Explosives
   (b) Diving (scuba)
   (c) Combat Tactics

4. September 1, 1961—Promoted to Lieutenant. Service number: 621051

5. <u>December 20, 1962</u>—Completion of active duty.

6. <u>July 5, 1964</u>—Recalled to active duty at U.S. Naval Amphibious Base, Coronado, California.

7. <u>July 4 to July 24, 1964</u>—Completion of Basic Parachutist Course, Fort Benning, Georgia.

8. <u>November 1964</u>—Completion of major course in the use of the MK6 (rebreather).

9. <u>September 1, 1966</u>—Promoted to Lieutenant Commander.

10. <u>January 3, 1967</u>—Completion of voluntary active duty with SEAL Team One. Received the following medals:
    (a) National Defense Service Medal
    (b) Armed Forces Expeditionary Medal (Vietnam)
    (c) Navy Commendation Medal with Combat "V"

<u>Key:</u>
I. OCS = Officer's Candidate School.
II. UDT = Underwater Demolition Team—Upon completion of UDT training on August 1, 1959, he was assigned as an officer to Underwater Demolition Team 12.
III. Combat "V" = Valor in Combat (Operations Piranha and Dagger Thrust)

Proposed Citation

The Commander in Chief, United States Pacific Fleet takes pleasure in presenting the NAVY COMMENDATION MEDAL to:

John Melvin STEPHENSON, Jr. Lieutenant, United States Naval Reserve

for service as set forth in the following:

"For meritorious service and performance of duty while serving as Officer in Charge, Underwater Demolition Team Twelve, Detachment BRAVO, and Commander Reconnaissance and Demolition Element, Amphibious Force, U. S. Seventh Fleet, during the period from 24 June 1965 to 10 October 1965. An extremely competent and courageous leader, Lieutenant STEPHENSON, while embarked in USS DIACHENKO (APD-123), was responsible during the above period for assisting in the detailed planning for and execution and analysis of the data obtained for each of numerous hydrographic surveys of the approaches to potential landing beaches along the coast of South Vietnam. Each of these survey operations was accomplished in a highly professional manner although hostile small arms fire was sometimes encountered. The results of these surveys contributed materially to the success of subsequent amphibious assault operations and areas best suited to provide maximum support for the resupply of logistical sites on the coast of South Vietnam. Lieutenant STEPHENSON invariably planned each operation in thorough detail and personally led his detachment to and in the objective area. The meritorious achievement and performance of duty that Lieutenant STEPHENSON displayed on survey operations was also evident during the two amphibious assault operations in which he directly participated. Operation PIRANHA during the period 5-12 September and Operation DAGGER THRUST during the period 20 September - 2 October 1965. In operation PIRANHA he led a detachment that performed a night clandestine beach survey immediately prior to the assault. In Operation DAGGER THRUST he led a detachment which successfully completed a similar survey in the face of enemy small arms fire. His outstanding leadership, judgement, courage and professional competence were in keeping with the highest traditions of the United States Naval Service."

Lieutenant STEPHENSON is authorized to wear the Combat "V".

```
                                                    FF-4/13/15:hs
                                                    1650
                                                    Ser
                                                    31 Mar 1966
```

From: Commander Amphibious Force, U.S. Pacific Fleet
To: Commander in Chief, U.S. Pacific Fleet

Subj: Personal Decorations and Awards; recommendations for

Ref: (a) CO, USS DIACHENKO (APD-123)

1. Reference (a) forwarded subject recommendation for personnel in USS DIACHENKO APD-123 as follows:

    a. <u>Navy Commendation Medal for meritorious service</u>

       John Melvin STEPHENSON, JR., Lieutenant, USNR, 621051/1105

2. Commander Amphibious Force, U.S. Pacific Fleet supports this recommended award for STEPHENSON, John Melvin Lieutenant, USNR.

                                            P. C. Dye
                                            Assistant Chief of Staff
                                            Administration and Personnel

Copy to:
COMSEVENTHFLT
COMPHIBAC
COMPHIBFORSEVENTHFLT
CO, SEAL ONE
CO, UDT-12
CO, USS DIACHENKO APD-123

THE NAVY SEAL

To Maxie Stephenson, the statements set forth below represented his perception of the Navy SEALs and life as an officer and operator in Naval Special Warfare. Several of these "Navy SEAL" cards were found in his belongings.

THE NAVY SEAL

"Make Love and War"   *"Better Bred than Red"*

AS SEEN BY

Shore Patrol / M. P. : A drunken, brawling, jeep-stealing, woman-corrupting liar, who wears a star sapphire ring, Rolex watch and K-Bar knife.

His Commanding Officer : A fine specimen of a fun-loving, athletic, provident, woman-appreciating improvisor, with a star sapphire ring and a Navy-issue Rolex watch and K-Bar knife.

Navy Department : An overpaid, overranked, insufferable tax burden, who is indispensable because he has volunteered to go anywhere and do anything, as long as he can booze it up, brawl, steal jeeps, corrupt women, lie and wear a star sapphire ring, Rolex watch and K-Bar knife.

Himself : A tall, handsome, highly-trained professional killer, female idol, sapphire ring-wearing, K-Bar knife-carrying gentleman who is always on time due to the reliability of his Rolex watch.

His Wife : A stinking member of the family who comes through Coronado or Little Creek about once every six months with a ruck sack full of dirty laundry and a hard-on...

Maxie Stephenson's Navy SEAL Badge

INDEX OF NAMES

Allen ("Bear Tracks") – 128
Allen, Richard ("Dick") – 53, 71, 127
Allred, Doug – 24, 45, 61
Antrim, Stan – 16, 141, 143
Balsarini, Don – 66, 67, 98
Barber, Dr. – 131, 132, 134, 155, 156
Barnes, Jim - 15
Bayer, Dr. – 155, 156
Bolen, Bugs - 120
Bowen, Ace - 125
Bower, Dr. - 156
Boynton, Mac ("The Pipe") – 62, 102, 107
Bramble, Dave – 36, 143
Brown, Charlie - 105
Bucher, Commander - 146
Burton, Chief - 135
Byrd – 32, 33, 34
Cait, Captain – 151, 152
Campbell, Rusty – 16, 28, 52
Carlin, Tommy – 105
Caroline – 93, 95, 97
Carroll, "Skinny" – 62, 116
Carse, Dave – 62, 84, 86, 98, 99, 105
Clancy, Chief - 16
Cobb, Petty Officer - 63
Cousin Weak Eyes – 124, 125
Crazy Amy – 125, 126
Cunningham, Danny - 62, 63, 102
Cunningham, H. O. – 13, 14, 16, 43, 74, 109

Del Giudice, Dave - 120
Doc – 71, 114, 115, 116, 117, 118
Dog, The - 103
Duncan, Admiral Charles K. – 150, 153
Early, Bill ("Buffalo Bill") – 67, 103
Fillmore - 98
Freeman, Clay – 79, 103
Fuller – 19, 27, 30, 39, 58
Gallagher, Prince - 62
Green, Frank - 98
Gruger, Chief- 9, 14
Happy Jack - 143
Hashmo, Commander – 143, 148
Hayes, Bob – 19, 29
Henry, Bob – 70, 114
Hiber, Harvey ("Klondike Ike") – 16, 40, 54
Hitler, Adolph - 147
Hoppy the Toad – 103, 104
Jones, Deacon - 128
Jurik, Fred - 62
Kenny, Jim – 24, 25, 33, 60, 61
Lanphier, Gary - 41
Lightfoot – 19, 53
Lion, The - 103
McNair, George ("Chicken") – 116, 117
McNalley, Paul -63, 83
Melnor, Eric ("The Hun") ("Fuck") – 62, 89, 90
Messinger, Joe ("Little Joe") - 32
Modesett, Tex - 62
Morrison, Chris - 62
Mosconi, Roger - 70
Murphy, Kevin – 16, 37, 38, 57, 58
Mussolini, Benito - 147
Old Smiling Jack – 143, 149

Parker, Mike ("Black Mike") - 16, 61, 142
Pearson, Mel ("Dirty Mel") ("Test Pattern Pearson") – 103, 104
Poppy, Hans – 19, 30, 38, 39
Price, Al ("Tree Trunk") – 16, 17, 59
Price, Lonny - 135
Ray, Aldo - 84
Reynolds, Ed - 73
Ruth, Herb - 137
Sansburn, Ken - 4
Savoy ("Survey") – 110, 111, 112, 113
Schmidt, John - 24
Schultz, Dale – 31, 32, 34, 40
Shenners, Charles - 96
Shirra, Wally – 110, 112
Skorzeny, Otto – 147
Smith, Ron - 42
Sonya ("Big Tits") – 90, 91
Spidone, Layton - 14
Stephenson, Janell – 4
Stephenson, MaryAnn - 41
Stephenson, Mel - 3
Storz - 96
Sudduth, Jack ("Whiskey Jack") – 62, 63, 102, 117, 129, 141, 142, 143, 144, 145, 148, 149, 150, 156
Texido, Bill - 24
Thurber, John - 13
Trader Vic - 116
Treolo, Gary - 102
Vias, Officer – 154, 155
Wagner, Wendy - 103
Weitzel, Rosemary - 2
Williams, Jim - 151

ABOUT THE AUTHOR

JOHN RANDALL STEPHENSON, ESQ. is an attorney and author who lives in Zephyr Cove, Lake Tahoe, Nevada. He is an avid skier, backpacker, and horseman.

The author is very grateful for the opportunity to finish and publish his father's stories that his father recorded so many years ago in the early 1970's and is grateful for the opportunity to share the stories with all readers of the book.

www.ingramcontent.com/pod-product-compliance
Lightning Source LLC
LaVergne TN
LVHW010325070526
838199LV00065B/5650